T0167949

Black and
Honolulu Blue

Black and Honolulu Blue

In the Trenches of the NFL

Keith Dorney

TRIUMPH
BOOKS
CHICAGO

Library of Congress Cataloging-in-Publication Data

Dorney, Keith.
    Black and Honolulu blue : in the trenches of the NFL / Keith Dorney.
    p. cm.
    Includes index.
    ISBN 1-57243-565-8 (hc)
    1. Dorney, Keith. 2. Football players—United States—Biography. I. Title.

GV939.D664A3 2003
796.332'092—dc21
[B]

                                                                    2003047329

This book is available in quantity at special discounts for your group or organization. For further information, contact:
Triumph Books
601 South LaSalle Street
Suite 500
Chicago, Illinois 60605
(312) 939-3330
Fax (312) 663-3557

Printed in the United States of America
ISBN 1-57243-565-8
Design by Patricia Frey

For Aud

Contents

Foreword

Leave it to an offensive lineman to write a book like *Black and Honolulu Blue.*

Offensive linemen are a unique breed. The only statistic that is kept on them is how many sacks they give up in a season—that is, unless you count how much they weigh, which nowadays is always in excess of 300 pounds. (Yeah, that's a strong selling point with the ladies.)

They are rarely mentioned by the press, they never get to run with or throw the ball (much less even touch it), and the only time they get their names announced over the loudspeaker is when they've committed a holding penalty.

I got to know quite a few offensive linemen while I was with the San Francisco 49ers, the Kansas City Chiefs, at Notre Dame, and back in high school in Pennsylvania and, quite frankly, I've always questioned their sanity. These are guys who go out and run full speed into a linebacker or sit back and let 300-pound defensive linemen crash into them. These are men willing to subject themselves to the sadistic training that they have to endure to be successful. During summer camp, when I glanced over at their sweaty, bloody, and dirt-stained bodies repetitively banging into one another in the mud, I often appreciated how intelligent I was when I chose to be a quarterback.

Oh, yeah, and I also count quite a few of them as my dear friends to this day.

The offensive linemen are usually the closest-knit group on the team, the hardest workers, and yes, with a few notable exceptions, some of the smartest.

I've also read quite a few football books in my day. Too often they repeat the same old themes, dwell on this big game or that, and explain in great detail what a great guy and tremendous football player the author was.

Let me tell you, this is not one of those books.

Keith Dorney speaks of the game from an in-the-trenches, gritty, and insightful perspective, quite unlike the fluff heard from commentators on television or sportswriters who have never played the game. That's what makes this book so entertaining, so fresh, and so compelling. Even if you're not the biggest of football fans, you'll have trouble putting it down. It is a fun, insightful, action-packed, and at times hilarious read, and it leaves you craving more at its conclusion.

There is something for everyone in *Black and Honolulu Blue.*

Young people will find it inspiring, even educational. It demonstrates what it takes to rise to the next level, make it to the big time, and become successful. It is a must-read for all aspiring athletes, no matter what the sport.

Women often find books in this genre boring and uninteresting—but that won't be the case with this one. Dorney captures what it's like to be the wife of a professional athlete—and let me tell you, it's not all money, fame, and eating bonbons in front of the television. He even writes about football mothers, and does so in an interesting and provocative way.

If you did play football—and the size of your heart is any bigger than a pea—then surely *Black and Honolulu Blue* will bring a tear to your eye. And I'm not just talking about professional football: if you played college, high school, or Pop Warner ball, or even if you're just one of those armchair quarterbacks with a beer in one hand and the remote in the other, you are going to love this book.

Also, consider the fact that *Black and Honolulu Blue* was written entirely by the guy who experienced it. Practically all sports books are written by a ghost author who invariably puts his own spin on things. But not this one—this is one of the few books about football that was written entirely by the same person who experienced the things being written about. When Dorney talks about getting a needle stuck in his knee to drain it of fluid before a game, about playing against some of the best defensive ends of all time, or explaining what it feels like to lose in the final seconds in the playoffs against the (ahem!) San Francisco 49ers, you know you're hearing the real story, right from the source.

Black and Honolulu Blue will touch your heart. You may never look at the game of football the same way again.

Not bad for an offensive lineman!

—Joe Montana

Acknowledgments

Ambitious undertakings, particularly daunting ones such as writing a book, come to fruition only through the efforts of many individuals. Football teams only succeed when a group of individuals mold their collective talents together toward a single goal. If my support group were a football team, surely we would have breezed through our division, gone on to the conference championship game, and soundly walloped our opponent in the Super Bowl.

However, there was no glory, stardom, riches, or "ring" to be had for my "teammates" on this project. In the beginning, like a division bottom dweller with limited talent and zero prospects, success appeared impossible and unrealistic—yet their enthusiasm and encouragement toward my lofty endeavor and their confidence in me never wavered. For that, I'm forever grateful.

First and foremost, the women in my life, a trio of remarkable ladies, deserve more praise than I could ever possibly bestow in a short paragraph.

Katherine, my best friend, lover, editor, and wife, has always made the worst days bearable, the good ones memorable, and the best of times legendary. She was there for me, transplanted from her native California, during my last trying years as a Lion, helping me weather those losing seasons, the coaching changes, and the inevitable injuries. Years later she was there again, this time as I struggled to find the right words to put down on paper. Her boundless encouragement, as well as her pointed critique and tireless editing, never wavered. Katherine, I will love you always.

Faye Dorney-Madgitz and I share the same persona, drive, and belief that anything in life is possible. We also share the same parents. My sister's tireless efforts on my behalf—editing, suggesting, and encouraging—were remarkable considering she runs her own business and has two school-age girls and a busy life of her own. Faye, those sacrifices, your unselfishness, and most of all your undeterred belief in me will never be forgotten. And thanks to Harvey, Kristen, and Jessica for their understanding as well.

My mother, to whom this book is dedicated, played the most integral of roles. She planted the love of writing within me early in life. It remained there for many years, lying dormant, waiting patiently for the day it would rumble, crack, and finally spring to life in an epiphany of realization. Although she has passed away, she remains with me and sometimes visits early in the morning when I'm alone with my words, gently embracing, loving, and comforting me. Those are the days I write my best.

If my mother was the planter, then Chester Aaron was the fertilizer. Most people would cringe at being called such a thing, but I know compost, manure, and pumice are as precious to him as a well-turned phrase. Initially, we met to talk of Creole Red, Purple Glazer, and Chinese Sativum. Our conversations now are more often about writing, although growing garlic, gathering wild mushrooms, and organic farming methods are always a part of our talks. Chester is the man who first suggested I write for others as well as myself. This exceptional man has done so many things in his life—he has been a writer, teacher, soldier, farmer, activist, and technician—but it is his encouragement and nurturing of writers, including me and countless others, that has been truly remarkable.

Bruce Henderson guided me through a myriad of obstacles—agents, publishers, proposals, and contracts—that finally led to the publishing of this book. Without him, surely it would still be in manuscript form, lying unread at the bottom of a pile on some editor's desk. Bruce, I know you'd rather see my next book published than accept my thanks, so I'll promise you here that I will do my best to make that happen. And thanks for keeping your fridge stocked with cold Pacificos for when I stop by.

Acknowledgments

Christine Walker, yet another Sonoma County writer friend, also spent time with my words, gently prodding me in the right direction, and I'm grateful to her for that—and to Dennis, too.

My father, Robert Dorney, has always supported me, no matter what the endeavor, and this book was no exception. Dad, I'm grateful for all you've done for me over the years.

I also want to thank Craig Dorney, who bestowed his love of sports on me, his kid brother. I probably never would have played football if it weren't for Craig.

And I can't forget two more Dorneys—Clayton and Alea—who put up with Dad and his sometimes crazy schedule. And Alea, how wonderful it was to wake up for an early morning writing session and find a note of encouragement from you, along with the coffee machine primed and ready to go. You guys are more important to me than anything, and I will always love you.

Thanks to Michael Emmerich, Blythe Hurley, Pat Castor (my baseball trivia guru), and my CYO basketball parent support group: Bob Erdman, Greg Lee, Dr. Drew, and Bobby Gonzalez.

This book was more about my teammates, coaches, and workout partners than it was about me, and without their colorful personalities it would have been boring as hell. Guys, this book was not only about you, it was also a tribute to you. Thanks to all of you for being a part of my life, giving me the experiences I wrote about, and sharing all of it—the good, the bad, and the indifferent—with me.

There are a few friends whose stories succumbed to the editor's pen: the Emmaus High School Green and Gold Hornets (Kenny Kissinger, Tony Kollar, Chuck Ayers, Richard Fritz, Dave Pennebacker, Bill Ternosky, Gary Crossley, Joel Koehler, Dave Bieler, Scott LeVan, Scotty Roeder, and Paul Mittura); the Allentown YMCA basement crew (Jeff Moyer, George Hummel, Carl "Buzzard" Emery, Dr. Bednar, Roger Katchur, Eskimo, and Cowboy); and the So Cal/Baja Contingent (Andrew Hammel and Larry Rodriguez).

Thanks to Tim Pendell and Bill Keenist of the Detroit Lions, who really went the extra mile for me. I also want to thank the following individuals, who unselfishly contributed their valuable time: Tim Curley, athletic director at Penn State; my fellow Macungie, Pennsylvania, friends, Dennis Fritz and Bob Young; Jack Hart and Sam Goldman of the East-West Shrine Game; and Pat LaFortune.

Chapter 1

Welcome to the NFL, Rookie

The sweat pouring down my face stung my eyes as I got down into my stance. I was in the midst of my first NFL practice, and I was confused, tired, and scared all at the same time. I struggled to remember the instructions given to me just moments before by my offensive line coach. The quarterback barked out the signals, the ball was hiked, and I set up into my pass-protection stance the best I could. Before I had a chance to react, or even process what I was supposed to do next, I was on my back. Dave Pureifory had just crashed into me and knocked me off my feet, then smashed his helmet into my chest as he drove me to the turf. He had hold of my neck with one giant hand and the front of my jersey with the other. He hesitated a moment, allowing his own sweat to drip through his mask and onto my face, then picked me up off my back slightly before once again slamming me back down to the turf.

"Welcome to the NFL, rookie," he said disgustedly as he walked away. I heard the laughter of the other veterans as I picked myself up and made my way back to the huddle.

I awoke but kept my eyes shut. I knew it was morning and time to get up—I could hear one of the staff banging on doors on the floor below, waking up the masses for the coming day. I was on my side facing the wall on my tiny single cot. The damp bedsheet stuck to my back, the result of yet another night of record-breaking heat and humidity. The fan I had purchased at the local KMart the week before whirred on, blowing the hot, humid air around the room. It was sweltering even at this early hour and smelled of dirty laundry, flatulence, and horse liniment.

I rotated my right ankle, then stopped. Yes, it was still sprained, but only enough to impede my performance and make my life miserable. My neck, sore from countless collisions with one behemoth freak of nature after another, shouted out at me as I painfully rolled to my other side. Maybe if I kept my eyes closed I wouldn't have to get up, go eat breakfast, and pad up for the upcoming two-hour-plus morning practice, which would again be held in conditions akin to Hades in summer. I wondered if the weather in Michigan was always this unbearable in July or if possibly the summer of 1979 was setting new records for heat and humidity.

I finally opened my eyes. My roommate was sitting on the edge of his bed, staring at me, his balls hanging out of his boxer shorts—not exactly the image you want to see first thing in the morning.

Welcome to Hill House, on the campus of Oakland University in Rochester, Michigan, and my first professional football camp.

My roommate was a nice enough guy, hailing from the University of Louisville. That's pronounced Loo-a-vul, by the way. My northern tongue had trouble enunciating it correctly, but he made sure he drummed it into my head over and over again until I got it right.

"That's Looavul, Keith, not Loo-is-ville, you dumb-ass Yankee."

We already had been through a lot together. We had endured four weeks of "pre–summer camp," which was held prior to the one of which we were currently in the midst. Each of those days had consisted of merely a single three-hour practice session, without football pads, during which our offensive line coach, Fred Hoaglin, had tried in vain to prepare us for the time when the veteran players would show up and we'd start practicing in earnest. However, nothing could have prepared us—short of Navy Seal training—for what we had been through these last three weeks. I was amazed when I realized we had only been sharing this room for a couple of months. It seemed more like an eternity. And we weren't even halfway through yet.

Waking up every morning with him staring at me was starting to become a bit disconcerting. Needless to say, he was beginning to get on my nerves.

He was beat up worse than I was, and the mental stress of it all had him near his breaking point, his behavior getting more bizarre as camp wore on. I should have been more tolerant, more compassionate, but those were trying times. In addition, I had my own problems.

When we first arrived, I was the one that was delusional, not him, and for good reason. First thing, the coaching staff tested our speed, strength, and endurance. My roommate ran a 4.8-second 40-yard dash; I ran a 5.1. He bench-pressed 455 pounds; I benched 395 pounds. He did 15 pull-ups; I did 11. He beat me by 200 yards in the 12-minute endurance run.

The Detroit Lions, with their precious first-round pick and a desire to shore up their offensive line, had chosen me with the 10th pick over all the other offensive linemen available in the draft. That was quite a billing to live up to, and I was determined not to disappoint them. But here was this undrafted free agent offensive tackle, from the University of Looavul, doing everything better than me.

I had felt the coaches watching me, probably wondering what the hell they were thinking when they chose me. Were they already regretting their decision? At that point, I was having some serious doubts about my future as a professional football player.

Once we put the pads on, however, everything had fallen into place. I knew how to play the game much better than my roommate, although I knew I still had a long way to go.

"How long have you been staring at me?" I asked.

"I don't know. An hour or so. I've been sitting here trying to figure out what you're doing that's so different from what I'm doing. I've been watching you on the field, too. I'm desperate. They're going to cut my ass next week if I don't figure this thing out soon."

Although every football camp I ever attended was hard work, this one was ridiculously difficult—exacerbated by several factors. Being "number one"—that's what a lot of the veterans called me—made me the center of attention, which I hated. The media was all over me, which was bad enough, but I was also the main focus of the Detroit Lions' defensive unit, which was downright painful.

I did have grounds for comparison. The very first football camp I ever attended was quite memorable in its own right. I was 14 years old, and in the part of Pennsylvania where I grew up, the high school freshman players attended camp with the rest of the football team. So, along with having to compete against my fellow ninth-graders, I would on occasion be lining up against a 19-year-old man who needed a shave. My 6'1", 130-pound body, which was still in the initial stages of puberty, made quite a target.

I vividly remember sitting in the back of John Hartzell's 1967 Rambler, Paul McCartney's "We're So Sorry, Uncle Albert" blaring loudly through the speakers on our way to one of our two-a-day practices. My time spent in the backseat of that car and in the backseat of Scott Stahl's 1968 Mustang and Dennis Fritz's blue 1964 Plymouth Fury (the boys, all seniors, took turns driving us from our homes in Macungie to the high school in Emmaus) was very special. That's because, given my druthers, I would have stayed there, curled up in the fetal position, avoiding yet another session where I was used as fodder for the seniors.

Yes, the similarities were there. I had no idea what I was getting into, I was outmatched both physically and mentally, and I was getting the living shit kicked out of me on a regular basis. But there was one big difference.

On one occasion, during the midst of that first high school summer camp, I fell asleep on the couch between practices and missed my ride. Those guys I mentioned were gracious enough to shuttle me back and forth to practice but weren't about to come looking for me. If I wasn't out on the street ready to go, they were gone. I tried in vain to hitchhike the five miles into Emmaus, but to no avail. I went back to my house in tears, dreading the next practice and the dire consequences I would surely have to face. The next morning, much to my surprise, no one said a word. I was just another face in a sea of over 60 freshmen trying out for football, and the coaches hadn't even noticed my absence.

Unfortunately, now there was no backseat to curl up on, no couch to hide out on, no mom to bring me a delicious lunch and dote on me. And I had the feeling that my absence might be missed if I decided to stay in bed this morning.

I got up and limped down the hallway to relieve myself in the communal bathroom. Every joint in my 21-year-old body ached. I had never been this stiff and sore in all my life, and I wondered how the hell I was going to endure the upcoming day, much less the upcoming weeks. We still had a long, long way to go. Plus, I was a bit unsettled about my roommate's peculiar behavior and wondered if I'd be able to sleep that night, envisioning him staring at me again from his bed.

Camp was tough enough, but I could only imagine what it was like with the threat of unemployment hanging over your head, the situation my roommate and countless others in the building were facing. I should have had more sympathy for him, but I was looking forward to the day when my double room became a single.

I limped back down the hallway to my room and started to get dressed in my standard camp gear—shorts, tank top, and thongs.

"I didn't sleep very well again last night," my roommate said in his Southern drawl. He showed me his elbow, painfully swollen to twice its normal size and still smelling of the DMSO he had applied the night before.

DMSO is a horse liniment that is illegal, at least for use on humans, and was just part of a cache of illicit and disputably effective supplies he had brought with him to camp, which he kept locked up in a briefcase. I wanted to point out to him that the use of some of these "supplements" might be the reason he wasn't sleeping at night, but I thought it best just to keep my mouth shut.

"How in the hell am I supposed to block that Pureifory with my arm in this condition?" he moaned, demonstrating the range of motion of his right arm, which looked to be close to zero.

"You figure it out—let me know," I countered.

Dave Pureifory, also known as "Orwell," "Low Rider," or one of a host of other nicknames he had inspired over his eight-year professional career, was the starting left defensive end for the Lions and the bane of our rookie class. Hell, he was the bane of anyone who lined up across from him.

The nickname Orwell had come from a character portrayed in an old Richard Pryor stand-up routine, dubbed by our other starting defensive end, Al "Bubba" Baker, a badass in his own right. Orwell was described by Pryor as the craziest, meanest, and downright nastiest brother in the hood, and that certainly rang true with Pureifory. If a vote was taken by the team to name the one person on the squad you did not want to fuck with, Pureifory would have won easily.

But I liked the nickname Low Rider the best. It described him perfectly. He stood only a little over six feet—puny by NFL standards. What he lacked in size, he made up for in quickness, agility, toughness, and dogged determination. His compact frame was thick and heavily muscled.

And he was tough—incredibly tough. I'm talking run-full-speed-into-a-brick-wall tough. The man started most days during the season by soaking his entire body in a tub of ice for a half hour at 7:00 in the morning. Tough. The year before, I was told, the Minnesota Vikings decided to run a quarterback option on Pureifory, with their quarterback Fran Tarkenton pitching the ball out to their running back at the last minute. Now, you have to wonder what the Vikings were thinking running the option with an 18-year veteran quarterback, but that's another story. Anyway, Pureifory smacked Tarkenton in the mouth so hard that he knocked out a good many of Fran's front teeth. The legend goes that Pureifory stood there laughing, right in Tarkenton's face, as the quarterback cussed him out, all the while spitting his broken teeth out onto the field. Really tough. It was rumored that a few years earlier, stricken with painful hemorrhoids but too embarrassed to approach the medical staff about them, he went ahead and removed them himself. Forget about the fact that the wound got infected and he had to be rushed to the hospital. Really, really tough.

And there were those eyes. He would look up at you from his stance with those big, wild, and crazy eyes, the whites of them always slightly bloodshot, accentuated by his dark, ebony skin. At the snap of the ball, he exploded off the line, a whirling, compact package of destruction.

Another rumor circulating around camp was that the year before he had stuffed a fellow 6'7", 270-pound defensive end into his locker, supposedly because he had asked to use Pureifory's comb. No one on the team messed with Pureifory, and that went double for rookies, whom he seemingly hated with all his soul.

The first two times I lined up against him during "individual pass rush"—a sadistic no-holds-barred drill that pitted an offensive and defensive lineman one-on-one against each other—I never even touched him. The ball was hiked, and before I got out of my stance, he was in the backfield annihilating the "quarterback"—a tackling dummy for the sake of the drill. The next time, I anticipated his quick upfield rush, set too far outside, and he again reached the tackling dummy untouched, this time to the inside. The third time I was so confused I didn't know what to do, so he flat ran me over, despite the fact that I outweighed him by 30 pounds. Later that day, he purposefully picked a fight with me during a scrimmage. I assumed that, for whatever reason, he hated me with a burning red-hot passion. I tried to act tough and unafraid, but deep down I was fearful he might kill me.

As my roommate and I walked across the campus to the cafeteria, the sky started to darken, taking on a slightly greenish hue, and the already impossibly thick humidity seemed to get worse.

"That looks like a tornado cloud," my roommate remarked, point-ing at a particularly nasty-looking cloud formation.

"If only we could be so lucky," I said.

Certainly we wouldn't practice during a tornado, would we? A tornado didn't postpone practice that day, but a few days earlier, we had been awakened in the middle of the night by Tim Rooney, our director of player personnel. He was going from room to room, getting everyone out of bed and to the basement for cover. Apparently, the next town over had just been hit by one.

I had listened to the blaring siren outside my window and the frantic warnings, then rolled over and went back to sleep. It would take a lot more than a tornado warning to get my pitiful butt out of the rack. Besides, I figured my chances of being killed were much greater out on the football field; the Detroit Lions' defensive line loomed much more dangerous than a mere act of God. And if a tornado did hit the building? I imagined myself being pulled out of the rubble, taken to a nice, clean hospital with pretty nurses, fresh sheets, and lots of bed rest, while my teammates practiced on in the relentless heat and humidity.

I huddled with a group of my fellow rookie offensive linemen during breakfast—we stuck together like wood rats for protection—and mulled over the day's schedule. Meetings, a two-hour-plus prac-tice, conditioning, lunch, more meetings, another grueling practice, dinner, then three more hours of meetings. That took us up to 10:00 at night, giving us a whole hour off before 11:00 bed check. Then we got to do it all over again. Day after day, for four more weeks.

"Are we going out for beer today?" inquired a free agent center from the University of Oklahoma.

"Damn right!" I replied enthusiastically.

A bunch of us had figured out the previous week that if we rushed off the field after the second practice, frantically ripped off our pads, tape, and equipment, and then took a cursory shower, we actually had time—a whole half hour, in fact—to go into town and grab a beer.

But what a half hour it was! That first beer never tasted so good. The second, third, fourth, and sometimes fifth weren't bad either.

"I vote for the Oceania," bellowed another rookie, this one a guard from West Virginia.

Ah, yes, the Oceania. Heaven could be such a place. The Japanese restaurant was close to camp, was dimly lit, and had the coldest beer in town. The owner had taken a liking to us and would actually put a case of beer in the freezer for us, anticipating our arrival at precisely the same time every day, like clockwork.

If we missed a day because of a change in venue—the local 7-Eleven for a cold quart—or a late practice, the owner would act offended, forsaken even, like a shunned lover. "You not come visit me yesterday. You come every day and then you not come. We miss you. Don't not come again!" he would chide us in broken English. As we weren't getting much appreciation anywhere else, we took it anywhere we could get it.

"The Oceania it is!" I wondered if getting excited about drinking beer at 7:30 in the morning—nine hours before the fact—was perhaps a little demented. Hey, whatever gets you through the day. Looking at the faces of my sorry-ass teammates sitting around the table, I knew I wasn't alone.

Our early morning warm and fuzzy beer fantasy was suddenly shattered. A fistfight broke out in the breakfast line, two linebackers apparently after the same bagel. The long days, heat, humidity, and mental stress were taking a toll on all of us.

"God, can't they at least wait until we get back out on the field?" I wondered out loud.

The harsh reality of the situation I was in didn't sit well with me. The intense competition, the kill-or-be-killed machismo of the NFL, which, if anything, was encouraged by the coaching staff, was new and foreign to me. I wondered if I would ever get used to it.

After breakfast, my roommate and I, along with our cadre of rookies, walked down to the locker room for a meeting with our position coach. Nothing was ever leisurely. If we weren't rushing to get our ankles taped before the meeting, we were desperately trying to memorize the six new running plays that were just put in for the upcoming practice.

The makeshift locker room was tiny, hot, and smelly. As I laced up my football spikes, sweat rhythmically dripped down off my nose. The half-tee I wore under my shoulder pads was already completely drenched. I drank a few cups of Gatorade before making the 200-yard walk down to the practice field. I took one last optimistic look at the clouds, but they were less menacing than they had been an hour ago.

"Monte's not going to allow it to rain, you big, dumb rookie," a voice said from behind me. It was Pureifory's distinctive baritone. I stopped and turned to face him, anticipating more rookie torture. Was I going to have to fight this crazy man here, before practice? I didn't have the energy and wished he would just leave me alone.

Instead, he explained to me head coach Monte Clark's divine powers over the weather and how he only allowed it to rain between and after practices. He said he couldn't remember the last time a practice was canceled because of the weather.

"Make sure you drink lots of liquids this morning, number one," he suggested, as he jogged off to join the mass of players already on the field.

His sudden somewhat friendly nature was puzzling. Was he being cordial so I would let down my guard, only to take advantage of my weakened defenses and pummel me into the turf later in practice? Paranoia overwhelmed me as I lined up in my usual place for our flexibility exercises.

As we concluded our stretching, the clouds parted, revealing a harsh and unrelenting sun that caused the temperature to climb into the high 90s, matching the stifling humidity. I took Pureifory's advice and downed more Gatorade, chased by several cups of water on the way to our individual drills.

During the next hour, several of my fellow rookie linemen, as well as other players both young and old alike, were carted off the field, victims of severe muscle cramping, the precursor to the life-threatening condition known as heatstroke. Players were falling like flies. However, coach Clark seemed pleased with the weather, pushing us harder and harder as the practice progressed, reminding us that we would be playing in conditions similar to this in our season opener in Florida.

Even though we had no control over cramping, everyone knew it was looked on as a sign of weakness by the coaching staff, so players tried to ignore the initial symptoms.

Football players around the country, from high school on up, die from heatstroke during summer workouts every year, a fact brought home recently with the publicity generated by the tragic death of Korey Stringer, an offensive tackle for the Minnesota Vikings.

First, one of the smaller muscles in your body starts to cramp, maybe a finger or toe. It's like your body is trying to say, "Hey, I'm burning up in here. Take off those ridiculous pads and go sit under a tree with a cold drink, stupid." If this early warning is ignored, the human body really starts laying down the law. Bigger muscle groups start to cramp, until you're eventually completely incapacitated and in some serious trouble. Severe dehydration, high body temperature, and possible death soon follow.

I received the warning signs on more than one occasion. I remember one time in particular. I took a step with my right leg and my quadriceps muscle cramped hard, sending me down to the ground in pain. In reaction to that movement, my left shoulder muscle went off, rolling me in the other direction, which in turn caused my abdomen to seize up. This necessitated immediate medical attention, especially since I was scaring the stewardesses with my screaming and blocking the aisle of the airplane on the flight home from our season opener in Tampa, where we played in temperatures of 95-plus degrees and high humidity.

Awareness of the killer that heatstroke is has come a long way. During two-a-day practices when I was in high school, the coaches would give us salt pills before practice, then deprive us of water until practice was over. We now know that sodium actually robs the body of fluid if not taken with lots and lots of water.

The only relief we got during those high school practices was midway through. Several five-gallon buckets of water were brought onto the field, and we would line up to get a quick splash in the face with a sponge. We would try and suck up as much liquid out of the sponge as possible when it was slapped in our face, despite the fact that we were sucking up our teammates' sweat, and God knows what else, out of those dirty, disgusting sponges.

A friend of mine, Matt Fitts, with whom I coached high school football at Cardinal Newman High School in Santa Rosa, California, told me a similarly disgusting story. Back at Lompoc High in Lompoc, California, they too were deprived of water during summer two-a-day practices. He discovered that there was always a residual amount of water left in the sprinkler pipes used to water the practice fields, and he would get down on his hands and knees, place his mouth over the sprinkler head, and literally suck as much of the stagnant, standing water out of the pipes as he could.

When your body needs water, it will do just about anything to get the liquid it craves, despite what the so-called experts of the time were telling us. At least now, in the NFL, we could drink as much water as we wanted.

It was time again for my favorite drill: one-on-one pass rush.

The little finger on my right hand started to cramp as I got down in my stance, once again facing my nemesis, Pureifory. I ignored the distraction, wanting not only to finally block him but to impress coach Clark as well, who was parked right in front of us. My offensive line coach barked out the signals, and I set up quickly on the snap. Pureifory tried his patented upfield speed rush, but I was ready for him and pushed him past the tackling dummy. On my next turn, he cut in front of the rookie defensive end who was next in line to face me. This time he tried to run me over, as he had so many times in the last few weeks, but again I was ready for him, viciously colliding with him and stopping him well short of the tackling dummy.

Pureifory grabbed me by the face mask and in frustration threw me down to the ground. Normally, I would have sat back and taken this rookie abuse, especially from one as menacing as Pureifory. But I, too, was nearing my breaking point and decided enough was enough. I grabbed his leg and tried unsuccessfully to body-slam him.

That was it. We both "threw down" and started to get it on. Both of us were furiously throwing punches at each other by the time we were separated by our teammates. Coach Clark stood nearby, stone-faced, taking it all in.

I remember glancing back at Pureifory as I walked back to my side of the field and getting a glimpse of those crazy, bloodshot eyes.

This is it, I thought. *I'm a dead man.*

I had one more turn left, and once again Pureifory jumped to the front of the line to face me. I tried not to tremble as I got down in my stance yet again, having no idea what he had in store for me. I overzealously set up too far outside. The wily Pureifory noticed my seemingly imperceptible mistake immediately and took a hard inside. I adjusted too late, and he beat me cleanly, murdering the tackling dummy. He added insult to injury by picking up the dummy, which weighed in excess of 50 pounds, and playfully throwing it at me as I walked away, hitting me in the back and nearly knocking me off my feet. This elicited laughter from everyone, including the ever-watchful coach Clark, adding to my embarrassment.

Clark called us all together after the grueling two-and-a-half-hour practice. I was exhausted and barely able to stand. We still had conditioning left—four "gassers," in which one gasser consisted of sprinting the width of the football field four times—plus the afternoon practice. I wasn't sure I was going to make it. At least I had made it through this one, though, and hadn't backed down from Pureifory's bullying.

"Men, you showed some real toughness in some very difficult conditions. It's hotter than two foxes fucking in a forest fire out here today, so how about we take the rest of the day off?"

After the cheering died down, he added: "Midnight curfew, and stay out of trouble. Remember, if anything bad happens, you left 10 minutes before it started. Now go out and have a good time. You've earned it."

It was our first night off in two and a half weeks, and it couldn't have come at a better time. My elation was short-lived, however. As I was leaving the practice field, Pureifory grabbed me roughly from behind by the arm, forcing me to stop and face him.

OK, I thought, *now he's going to kill me.* That's when he surprised me.

"Don't come out toward me on your pass set," Pureifory said. "Set straight back. If you had set straight back that last time I never would have been able to beat you to the inside. And get your hands out on me like this." He grabbed both of my wrists and showed me exactly what he meant.

He spent the next half hour with me, first walking through the moves then demonstrating full speed, explaining eloquently along the way exactly what he meant. He revealed to me how he thought I could best block him. Then he explained to me the finer points—from a defensive lineman's perspective—of playing offensive tackle in the NFL.

I noticed coach Clark eyeing me like a proud father. It seemed he knew that Pureifory would dog me unmercifully until I stood up to him. That small sign of approval really meant a lot to me because this was a guy who knew a little bit about playing tackle in the NFL. He had blocked for the legendary Jim Brown, battled with the likes of Bubba Smith, and helped win championships while playing that position for the Cleveland Browns in the sixties. Furthermore, he coached the offensive line for Don Shula during the Miami Dolphins' salad days in the seventies. His first stint as a head coach was with the San Francisco 49ers, and he probably would have retained that job were it not for a new up-and-coming coach named Bill Walsh, who replaced him in 1977. Now, in his second stint as a head coach, he was personally making sure his first-round draft pick, his protégé, was going to be successful.

I felt like I had somehow graduated to another level, like Jonathon Livingston Seagull on his way to the next plateau or Grasshopper finally snatching the pebble from his master's hand.

"And relax. You're doing fine," Pureifory added, as we walked off the field together. "Don't think you're going to learn everything at once. You're going to be a great offensive tackle in this league for a long time."

He jogged away, leaving me standing there in a temporary state of shock. I felt rejuvenated—alive. And it was precisely at that moment that I knew, for the very first time, that I was not only going to survive that camp, I was going to be an NFL football player.

I never knew what became of my old roommate. The Lions released him at the end of the following week, and I never saw him again. I remember his elbow got even worse, but he stoically practiced on, knowing that if he tried to take a few days off and let it heal some, the Lions would have cut him even sooner. It was a woeful situation to be in, but he handled it like a man. He was a tough guy, a hard worker, and a good friend for the short time I knew him. When he finally was released, I could tell he was relieved but disappointed, wanting to stick with the team as long as possible despite the tremendous pain he was enduring because of that elbow. He said his good-byes to me and the other remaining rookie offensive linemen, packed up his car with his meager belongings, and headed back down I-75 towards Looavul.

Wherever you are, my friend, I wish you well. That goes for all the other nameless fellow rookies that I remember so clearly from that summer. It was a long time ago, but in a lot of ways it seems like it was just yesterday. I will never forget that time we spent together. Ever. Ridiculously difficult situations, like that first camp, are forever entrenched in my memory.

As it turned out, Pureifory and I ended up becoming good friends. For years we lined up against each other in practice, working hard and making each other better. Before every game in warm-ups, we'd get together for one monstrous hit—"to clear out the cobwebs," he liked to say—a hit that would resonate throughout the stadium. Although he was a very private person, it turned out we shared many common interests.

For the next few years, I sat back and enjoyed watching Pureifory torture whole new sets of rookies. I'd let them find out for themselves that their tormentor was actually an intelligent, educated, and thoughtful person, who had not only a college degree, but a post-graduate one as well, a fact kept secret from most of his teammates.

Years later, long after Pureifory had left the Lions, I was watching television during the off-season, clicking through the different channels. I stopped momentarily on a USFL football game. Remember the USFL? Its motto, "pro football in the spring," never really caught on, and it folded after a few years back in the early eighties. But there was Pureifory, well into his thirties, sacking the quarterback, playing for some team from Birmingham, Alabama. I watched the rest of the half, commiserating with that poor offensive tackle who was unsuccessfully trying to block him. Pureifory must have had four sacks against him, and that was just the one half. Once a badass, always a badass.

As for me that year, my first in the NFL? Well, I ended up surviving—just barely—despite Pureifory's bullying, my roommate, and the rest of the rookie torture I had to endure. I ended up starting every game, and if I remember correctly, played every single offensive down, both in the preseason and regular season, coach Clark wanting me to gain as much experience as possible in my first year. That's the good news. The bad news is we ended up having the worst season in Lions history, going a miserable 2–14, punctuated by an inept offense that featured a terrible running attack and an even worse passing game. To make matters worse for me, a fellow rookie hit me with a beer mug in a bar fight near the end of the year, fracturing my cheek-bone and giving me 70 stitches just under my left eye. That happened on a Thursday before a Sunday game in Philadelphia, and I'm proud to say I played anyway, even though every time I hit All-Pro defensive end Claude Humphrey that day it felt like a giant tuning fork was going off inside my head.

We learned from our mistakes, drafted some key players, and subsequently fielded some pretty good football teams during the rest of Monte Clark's tenure. Monte was a great coach, easily the best I ever had in the NFL, and I'm proud to have played for him. We were close—real close—to having a championship team during those years, but unfortunately for all of us, it was not in the cards.

One thing never changed, though. I always hated summer camp. Anyone who tells you that they like summer camp is either a liar, crazy, or both. Ask any football player who's endured even one, at any level.

You've heard the old saying: "What doesn't kill you makes you stronger." I guess that can be said about all those summer camps I endured. They made me a better football player. They helped build my character. Most of all, though, they gave me memorable moments that I will keep with me for the rest of my life, that I can replay in my head over and over again.

Often during the football season, I wish I was young again and able to go pad up and play some football. On the other hand, I never, ever, once wished I was in the middle of six weeks of summer camp. When you're a football player, I guess you have to take the good with the bad.

And thank goodness this summer I don't have to go through another one!

Chapter 2

Broken Bones!

"Get the fuck off of me. Get the fuck *off* me, man," I pleaded
with the bodies lying on top of me. They quickly complied,
and I lay there on the AstroTurf holding my left leg,
hollering bloody murder. I had no idea what had just
happened; one minute I'm blocking my man, the next minute
I'm down there screaming like a big baby. My ankle hurt more
than anything, but the rest of my leg felt strange, too.

After regaining some level of composure—at least I had
stopped yelling—I assessed that I had sprained my ankle
somewhat and had just overreacted terribly to what was
surely just a minor injury. Embarrassed by my outburst
but still in agonizing pain, I quickly got up and tried
jogging down to where Leonard Thompson had just caught
a pass for a first down.

"Son of a bitch!" I moaned, limping badly on the leg, still
trying to figure out what the hell had just gone down. I
wasn't sure which was worse now, my ankle or my knee. At
this point there was just a general pain emanating from
the whole leg, and it felt numb when I put weight on it. I
reluctantly veered off to the sideline, passing my backup,
who had already been sent in for me.

"Damn it, damn it, damn it!" I cried, as I ripped the helmet off my
head, throwing it down hard with both hands onto the AstroTurf in
frustration. The impact caused most of the pads inside it, secured by
either velcro or metal snaps, to fly off in all directions. An equipment

manager immediately ran out onto the field and started gathering up the mess. When I reached the sideline, I was met by our head trainer, Kent Falb, who grabbed me firmly by the elbow and guided me over to the end of our bench, where team orthopedic surgeon Dr. Robert Tiege was waiting.

"I think it's my knee. And my ankle. Shit!"

For the first time all year, my feeling of indomitability started to falter. During the last two seasons, despite an almost constant onslaught of injuries occurring all around me, I had begun to feel invincible. I think your brain does that to you after a while, probably as a defense mechanism. The constant carnage, in both games and practices, was almost too much for the conscious mind to bear.

I was in the midst of my 22nd consecutive regular-season start for the Detroit Lions, and up to this point, I hadn't missed a down. The fact that our offense was out there on the field doing battle against the New Orleans Saints' defense without me at right tackle was almost too much to bear. It didn't sit well with me, despite my pain.

I sat there on the bench red-faced, sweat pouring off me, instinctively trying to peer over my teammates lining the sideline and catch a glimpse of the continuing action on the field. *I should've stayed out there*, I thought, as Dr. Tiege grabbed my leg, secured my ankle firmly in his right armpit, and gently tested the knee's stability by pushing on the sides of my upper calf in a back and forth motion.

My attention shifted back to my leg as I instinctively flexed my quadriceps and hamstring muscles to protect myself against any more pain, which was flowing from the leg in general, not from any one specific place.

"I can't tell anything about your knee now," Tiege explained in his laid-back, soft-spoken tone. "You're too tensed up. Let's take a look at the ankle."

As Tiege placed my leg down on the bench, the three of us simultaneously looked at it. No one had to say a thing. Despite the two layers of socks and a heavy tape job, there was already noticeable swelling on the outside of the ankle. Tiege started to try and test it by picking the leg up and moving my foot back and forth, much like he had done with my knee, but then thought better of it.

"Look, you obviously have a pretty serious sprain there. I'm not going to mess with it now and cause you any more pain."

"Tweety, tape it up before it swells any more," I said. Tweety looked over at Tiege, who shrugged his shoulders, frowning.

I wasn't used to calling Falb "Tweety." It was still a novelty. Nearly all of the older veterans addressed him by that nickname, and I was tired of being treated like a rookie. It was my second year now. I had been testing the waters the last few months, slipping in a "Thanks, Tweety" after he finished taping my ankle and a "Morning, Tweety" after reporting for treatment. He hadn't seemed to mind.

Falb, trainer for the Detroit Lions the last 15 years, didn't let just anyone call him by his nickname. Compared to the giants he dealt with on a daily basis, the diminutive, bespectacled, and soft-spoken Falb did look a bit like his cartoon counterpart. But you had to first gain his respect before you called him Tweety to his face. Pity the poor rookie who unknowingly blurted out a casual but unearned "Hi, Tweety."

Tweety had seen a lot in his years with the Lions. He had a man die in his arms. Chuck Hughes, a Lions wide receiver in the early seventies, suffered a heart attack and passed away on the field in a game against the Chicago Bears. In one of the more heart-wrenching moments in NFL history, many will remember Dick Butkus' impassioned pleas for help as he stood helplessly over his fallen opponent. Tweety was first on the scene. He'd also been there for injuries that caused permanent paralysis. And, of course, he had tended to countless blown-out knees, compound fractures of the leg and arm, and more sprains, contusions, and head trauma cases than an emergency room doctor.

We all turned our heads and looked up at once. Head coach Monte Clark was making his way over to us. Suddenly, his forward progress stopped and his head jerked backward, much like a dog coming to the end of his leash. His headset cord had caught on someone's foot. He stopped, turned, and yanked hard on the cord with both hands, freeing up enough slack to make it over to us, tripping up several unsuspecting players in the process.

At 6'7" and 300 pounds, with size 17 triple E feet, Monte Clark didn't sneak up on anybody. He walked heavily yet quickly over to us. If there was any concern on his face, it was overshadowed by the stress that was so evident on it. His eyes, wild and darting, were accentuated by the big bags under them, the result of film sessions long into the night, every night, deep in the bowels of the Pontiac Silverdome. His jowls, long and creased, gave him a bulldog-like appearance. His hair was generously peppered with gray, even though there had not been a speck of it present when I'd first met the man a year and a half before. His work habits were starting to become legendary, but at that moment the three of us could clearly see they were taking a heavy toll on him.

"What do we got?" he asked no one in particular. Tweety had already begun taping the ankle, this time directly over my shoe and sock.

"Give me another minute," Tweety said, as he ripped off another piece of white tape. The speed and accuracy of his movements, honed by the taping of literally hundreds of thousands of ankles before this one, were incredible, his arms and hands a blur as he hollered at a subordinate for my helmet.

I looked up at Monte and nodded, his icy-cold stare telling me, in no uncertain terms, that unless something was seriously broken, torn, or ripped, I had better get my ass back out there on the field. I swallowed any doubts I had about returning to the game, along with a bile-filled burp, and grabbed my helmet, limping back onto the field to join our offensive huddle. My teammates had driven the ball down to the 20-yard line, and with any luck we could punch it in and put this thing away.

Even though my mobility was greatly reduced and I was in tremendous pain, I hobbled through the rest of the game, barely making it to the final whistle. No one was happier to have that game over than me. I sat exhausted in front of my locker, choosing not to participate in the jubilant celebration around me. We ended up winning, 24–13, despite my less than peak fourth-quarter performance and two offside penalties, which were the result of my trying to compensate for my condition. Sure, I was glad we had just boosted our record to 5–1, putting us atop the NFC Central Division, but I had some serious concerns about my health.

The sweat still flowed from me. Every piece of my clothing, padding, and equipment had long since been drenched by it. I smelled heavily of cigarette smoke. Even though smoking at your seat in the Silverdome was illegal, tens of thousands of butts were lit up that afternoon, and the smoke, trapped inside the fully enclosed dome, saturated everything in it with its thick, acrid smell. Teammate Dave Pureifory liked to say he felt like a canary in a coal mine on Sunday afternoons, and at that moment I knew exactly what he meant.

I leaned forward to cut the tape from around my left ankle. Beads of sweat rhythmically dripped off my nose onto the Honolulu blue carpet. Two hundred and eighty pounds before the game, I now weighed less than 260, a water weight loss of over 20 pounds.

Removing my jersey, specially tailored to fit my shoulder pads, arms, and torso like a glove, seemed like an impossible task at the moment. I instead grabbed a trainer's pair of scissors out of my locker and cut the straps of my shoulder pads that ran underneath my armpits, allowing me to lift the pads and jersey off together over my head rather than having to wrench the jersey separately over the pads.

Five distinct red marks formed a semicircle on my neck right below my three-day-old beard stubble. That's where Elois Grooms had grabbed me after missing on an arm over. He instead grabbed me by the neck and tried to push my head downward in his attempt to sack our quarterback. I had bent my knees, dropped my butt, and let his fingernails rip into me, gladly trading a few scratches and bruises for the thwarting of his pass rush.

I finally got everything off me and started limping naked toward the showers. I was going to be in the training room for a while and figured I might as well take a shower before going in there. That's when I remembered Kip. My good buddy and teammate from college, Kip Vernaglia, was visiting that weekend, and I had told him that if we won I'd come and get him out of the tunnel and bring him into the locker room. I found Mark Glenn, our assistant equipment manager at the time, nearby. He had met Kip at practice the day before, and I asked him if he'd go fetch him for me.

"Thanks, Mark. I really appreciate it. Just sit him near my locker."

"No problem, man," he answered, just as both double doors burst open and a throng of media types, led by a shapely redheaded television reporter, poured into the room.

"Whoops." I turned and started walking back toward the showers, exposing my backside to the crowd. What was I going to do? Like everyone else, I was still getting used to having women in the locker room after the game. It was a new phenomenon that was here to stay, though, and I had better get used to it.

"Kiss my big hairy white butt," I muttered, as I turned into the communal shower area and out of view. All the showers were occupied, the loud din amplified by the narrow, tile-covered walls. Steam from the hot water somewhat obscured the muscular bodies, tight asses, and ample dicks that danced and swayed in front of me. If we had lost, all you would have heard was the sound of running water.

"Jesus Christ, number one, if you were any whiter I'd need some damn sunglasses," a big defensive end joked, eliciting laugher from everyone within earshot. "Get your big ass in here, bro." He grabbed me by the back of the head with a big paw and guided me under his shower, then disappeared off into the mist.

I stepped into the water stream, wincing as it stung the many raw abrasions that covered my body. Normally I would meticulously wash with antibacterial soap every open cut—the Pontiac Silverdome's dirty, fetid AstroTurf surface was a harbinger of bacteria, and staph infections were all too common—but I just wasn't in the mood. Plus, my pain threshold had dropped to zero. During the game you could have run a Mack truck over me and I wouldn't have felt a thing. But battling through the pain of my leg nearly the entire second half had exhausted me, and I just couldn't stomach any more of it.

I finished my cursory shower, wrapped a towel around my waist, still wary of the redhead, and headed back to my locker. I noticed that Kip not only was in the locker room but was entertaining a group of linebackers, usually a tough audience, a few lockers over. That was my buddy Kip. Everyone instantly liked him, wooing anyone within his vicinity with his dark Italian good looks, easygoing manner, and heavy northern New Jersey accent.

A *Detroit Free Press* beat writer immediately appeared, throwing his handkerchief up in the air, obviously in reference to my two offsides penalties. Despite our win, I was in no mood for teasing, especially at the hands of this fat little weasel, and the anger that was with me for most of the game returned immediately. I wouldn't have thought his little skit was funny even if the penalties weren't the result of my overcompensating for my injury. Of course, he didn't know I was playing hurt, but I didn't care.

"Fuck . . . you," I said slowly and deliberately, at the same time poking my broken, twisted right index finger into the lapel of his cheap, poorly fitting sports coat. My face was already flushed red with anger, and his previously cheerful expression immediately melted from his face.

"God damn it, Dorney, lighten up," he said, as he took two big backward steps away from me. "By the way, can I quote you on that?" he said, trying to make light of the encounter as he walked even farther away from me. I stared at him angrily as he turned his back to me, no doubt seeking out a less dangerous interview.

I hated that little prick in particular. He never had anything good to say about the Lions, and I was sure he was rooting against us that day, hoping his prediction of a midseason Lions collapse would finally come true. I made a mental note to quit reading the sports page.

"Geez, Dorn, dazzling the media with some colorful quotes?" It was Kip, and I couldn't help but laugh along with him.

"What the hell was that all about?" inquired Kip.

I dismissed the sportswriter with a wave of my hand. "That asshole's going to write whatever he feels like, despite anything I say."

"Hey, how's your wheel? Are you OK?"

By the time I explained the situation to him and told him I was probably going to be a while, we had already set him up with a few of my teammates, who were more than happy to usher him around Detroit for a night of celebration.

"You're gonna hook up with us later, right? You know where we'll be?"

"I'll find you guys, Kip. Have fun, man."

"Don't worry about your homeboy, number one. We are going to show him how we party in Motown, baby!"

I already knew my ankle was wasted, but it was my left knee I was now most worried about. It had stiffened up on me considerably, just in the last few minutes. I gingerly limped off to the training room.

The training room, directly adjacent to the locker room through a set of double doors, was rectangular, as long as the locker room but only a fourth as wide. Two rows of high, skinny tables, two-and-a-half feet wide by seven feet long, lined each side of one end of the room, their short ends butting against each side of the wall, forming an aisle between each of them. The trainers' offices and the doctor's examination room, sealed off from the rest of the training room by a wall of glass, lay beyond the tables. Most of the tables were occupied by large, burly men, celebrating loudly despite their injuries, in various stages of undress, ice bags strapped to shoulders, elbows, knees, and ankles.

As soon as Tweety saw me, he stopped what he was doing and ushered me back to see Dr. Tiege. I waited and watched as he attended to a wide receiver's broken jaw. He, too, had the injury occur in the third quarter and, like me, had played the remainder of the game. He would get it wired shut the next day and play that way for the next six weeks, protected by a bulky shield that fit underneath his helmet. That shield would protect his jaw somewhat from further injury but severely limit his breathing and vision and, unfortunately for him, call attention to it. Next Sunday he might as well wear a big neon sign on his head reading "Hit Me Here," pointing to his busted jaw. That injury would be listed on our next opponent's scouting report, you could be sure of it. I wasn't the only one on the team with a problem.

Dr. Tiege was his own man, which wasn't easy when you're the orthopedic surgeon for an NFL football team. Everyone was always trying to tell him what to do. Pressure came from management, the coaching staff, and the players, all trying to manipulate the decisions he had to make on a daily basis. Careers often hung in the balance.

I believe there is one reason and one reason only why he put up with all of the bullshit, why he hadn't yet scrapped this job for some cushy practice where he could treat old men with racquetball injuries for a lot more money. It had nothing to do with money or prestige, and it certainly wasn't because of the Michigan weather. It's the same reason why the U.S. Ski Team moves to Chile during the summer, why surfing legend Tom Curren lives by his favorite beach break, and why the expert angler resides by a wild trout stream. Nowhere else would he be able to operate on and rehabilitate such gruesome injuries. Even though he was born and grew up in California and could start a practice there tomorrow if he wanted, he had chosen to live in a suburb of Detroit, Michigan, to be close to this never-ending stream of horrific orthopedic injuries. The man was into what he did.

With a soft, gentle voice he called me over to the treatment table, and I sat down on it, my legs out in front of me. My right leg lay straight out on the table. The left leg, although straightened as far it would go, was still bent at the knee, not even close to the right leg's "locked-out" position.

He frowned, moving around the table silently, examining me with his eyes only, not bothering to touch what he knew was still a dreadfully sore leg. His face was solemn. I tried to read what he was thinking but instead got distracted by one of his wild, untamed eyebrow hairs, which was protruding out at an odd angle. I was still focused on that stupid eyebrow hair when he stepped back, obviously searching for the right words to say. Tweety, ever present, laid a gentle hand on my calf, between my dual injuries, as if to calm me for what was about to be said.

"Keith, I'm really just guessing at this point, mind you. You've probably got a second-degree medial collateral ligament sprain, possibly some damage to your meniscus cartilage." He paused, crossing his arms, then reached up with his right hand to hold his chin. He knew what I wanted to hear and was searching for the right words to soften the blow somewhat.

"There is no way I can tell for sure now. Certainly, given the fact that you played the rest of the game, I would say the chances of it being any more serious than that are minimal. I don't like all that swelling, though, but I guess that can be expected, given the circumstances."

He turned his focus to the ankle, picking it up, again examining it without yanking, twisting, or pulling on it, keeping any pain he caused me to a minimum. He frowned as he put my leg back down on the table.

"That's a nasty outside ankle sprain you have there, but I doubt it's anything worse than that. We had better get it X-rayed just in case, though." He paused once again, folding his arms, massaging his chin with his right hand.

Tweety and I exchanged glances, then focused back on the doc.

"I want to take a look inside of the knee first thing tomorrow morning. It's not going to be a very invasive procedure. Hopefully I'll have you back to work by Wednesday, and with any luck, you'll have a chance of playing next week."

At first I was surprised to hear that he was even talking about me playing in next week's game. I was more concerned at the moment about how I was going to make it up the ramp to my van. Thinking about next week's opponent at this point was too much for me to comprehend.

"It's possible that we might find some more extensive damage in that knee. There's really no way of telling without taking a look. You quite possibly might end up worrying more about that ankle than anything else."

I looked over at Tweety for some type of confirmation, but his face was still rather grim and serious. I was confused. What had he just said? Did he say he was going to operate on my knee tomorrow? His casual tone and choice of words made it sound more like we were going down to Detroit for a burger and a movie the next day rather than to perform major knee surgery.

Arthroscopy had been around for a while but really was still in its infancy; however, Tiege was a pioneer in the field and was comfortable performing more and more intricate procedures with it. To him, it really wasn't a big deal.

"So you're going to operate on my knee tomorrow?" Both men stared back at me in silence.

"Are you going to have to put me out, or can you just numb the leg?" I asked. It was my understanding that every time they knocked you out with those drugs to perform surgery, drugs that would normally kill you except for the respirator and other equipment they hooked up to you, it literally stripped years off your life.

"Yes, Keith, we'll have to put you out for this one, I'm afraid. But it should only be for a short while, and the effect from it should be minimal."

"Can't you just numb me up like last time? I don't need to watch, unless of course you don't mind."

Earlier that year, Tiege had performed his first surgery on me. My left thumb had gotten caught in an opponent's face mask and was sticking straight up in the air, perpendicular to the other fingers, when I came off the field. They had just numbed my arm for that one. At my request, he had even let me watch part of the procedure.

"No one has ever asked to watch before," I remember him saying. I think that's when we first started to become friends. I was into what he did, and he respected that, just like I respected him for appreciating the fact that I had played the week after, only missing a few practices because of the surgery.

"Not for this one, Keith. And that's why you'll need to get down to Henry Ford as soon as you can. First thing tomorrow means approximately 12 hours from right now," he said, glancing at his watch. "That way you'll have even more time to heal before next week's game."

Man, enough about next week's game, I thought, as I limped back out to what was now a nearly empty locker room. I gathered my things and headed outside. It took me a good 15 minutes to make it to my customized Ford Econoline van, parked 200 yards away and up a steep incline from the locker room.

As I headed down Woodward Avenue toward the hospital in Detroit, the reality of my situation finally began to sink into my thick skull. Here I was, alone in a strange city, facing what could be a career-threatening injury. I thought of my mom and dad. Should I call and tell them? I wished at that moment that Kip would have stuck around. I was scared, really scared, and could use someone to talk to right now. I looked around at the hundreds of people in their cars—strangers, all of them—oblivious and uncaring as to my plight.

Back at the Silverdome, unbeknownst to me, coach Clark was already watching film of the game. He swore to himself there in the dark, then ran the play back a few more times just to be sure. He wasn't a doctor, but he had seen enough blown-out knees in his day to know he had just lost his starting right offensive tackle for the year. He cringed as he watched the bodies fall against my leg, noting my left foot firmly planted on the unyielding AstroTurf. The angle at which my left leg bent under those falling bodies—an angle no leg could achieve with a properly attached medial collateral knee ligament—momentarily made him sick to his stomach.

I arrived at Henry Ford Hospital and spent the night, alone, in my private room. Henry Ford's grandson, William Clay Ford Jr., owned the Detroit Lions, in addition to a big chunk of Ford Motor Company, and the Ford family was still a major benefactor of the hospital. Almost all of the team's surgeries were performed here. It was right in the heart of Detroit, a good hour's drive from the Silverdome in Pontiac, far away from our homes and workout facilities. With all the unfamiliar surroundings and faces, I felt isolated and removed, which only helped compound my fears.

It was a long, lonely night, and I barely slept.

They first came at 5:00 in the morning and, silently, with no explanation, stuck a needle in my arm and set up an IV. An overzealous male nurse, who had just shaved my leg all the way up to my ass, was attempting to shave my pubic area as well.

"They're scoping me down here, at the knee. Why in the hell would you need to do *that*?" I protested.

"I'm just doin' my job. It's standard procedure," he said, as he started to try and lift up my hospital gown. Just then Dr. Tiege, accompanied by his entourage, walked into the room. His gentle smile and demeanor immediately put me at ease. It was the first familiar face I had seen since leaving the Silverdome the night before.

He quietly told the nurse that what he had already shaved was sufficient and sent him on his way.

"I'm just doin' what I was told," he said angrily as he stormed off.

This elicited chuckles from the entourage, but Dr. Tiege was all business. He raised his eyebrows as he looked at the badly swollen knee and the even more swollen ankle, which by now had also turned a nasty shade of black and blue.

"Well, the X-rays we took last night don't show anything, so that's good news," he said as he covered my leg back up with the sheet and blanket. "You doing alright?"

"As well as can be expected."

"Well, it will all be over soon, and you'll be as good as new. See you down in the OR." They left as quickly as they had arrived, leaving me alone with my fears.

Shortly afterward I was transferred to a mobile gurney and wheeled to another part of the hospital, where they injected something into my IV that they said would "relax" me. And relax me it did. In fact, I was downright happy and actually started enjoying myself, despite the circumstances. Again they moved me, this time leaving me in a hallway connecting all of the operating rooms.

From my vantage point, it appeared I was lying inside a steel cage. The side rails, colored the same metallic gray as the gurney to which they were attached, contained me, my shoulders rubbing up against them. My bare feet hung out over the end, the sheet not quite making it over the rise of my long, skinny feet.

Through the bars I could see men and women dressed in pinkish-maroon uniforms hurrying past me almost continuously, their faces grim and serious, avoiding any eye contact.

After what seemed like an inordinate amount of time—I couldn't be sure of anything after the drugs they had given me—I began shivering uncontrollably under the single sheet that didn't quite cover me. They had tucked the sheet underneath my arms and legs on each side, encasing me, and I was unable to move anything but my feet and head.

I wasn't happy anymore. I started to get a little claustrophobic, and I was freezing. Just then Tiege's people arrived, the same ones that were in my room earlier. The lone woman in the group asked me if I was OK, and I said I was fine except I was freezing to death.

She immediately went and retrieved a couple of warm blankets, tucking one of them underneath and around my bare feet and placing the other over the top of me, gently tucking the end of it underneath my chin.

"Is that better?" she asked in a motherly tone.

"Yes, yes, it really is—thank you." I was back to being happy again. They wheeled me into the operating room, transferring me onto the single table in the middle of the room. I was fascinated by all of the shiny chrome fixtures, the bright lights, the efficiency with which everyone moved. I temporarily forgot why I was there, and I blabbered on, the cheerful but serious staff answering all of my many questions.

Dr. Tiege came in a few moments later, and immediately all conversation ceased, except for me. I chattered on, oblivious to my dire circumstances, still high and happy from the hospital-grade opiates. Tiege looked very comfortable, more at ease here than I had ever seen him. It was then that I realized that he was in his element. This was *his* world, just as the locker room and football field were mine.

The respect his team gave him as he prepared for surgery was evident, and I knew right then and there that I couldn't have been in better hands. The anesthesiologist injected yet more drugs into my bloodstream through my IV, and I could feel them burning in my veins as he told me to start counting backward from 100. I cheerfully and inappropriately told everyone "good luck" and started counting. I didn't make it past 97.

The next thing I remember, I was flying effortlessly over a lush green landscape, not a care in the world. My arms were outstretched like a big bird of prey, the sun warm on my bare back, the wind cool and refreshing against my naked body.

I dipped low along the tree line, then soared upward, higher and higher, my speed slowing until I was suspended momentarily in the air before allowing gravity to overtake me. As I started hurtling faster and faster toward the ground, panic replaced the serenity, as fast and as sudden as light leaves a windowless room after throwing the switch. I began kicking, grasping, flailing wildly with my arms and legs, trying desperately to regain my power of flight.

My conscious senses flickered back, and I instantly perceived I was now in a horrible place, a place far, far away from where I had just been, from where I had just fallen from the sky like a rock. Pain, incredible pain, roared to life, and a wave of nausea overcame me. I was retching, choking, gasping for air. When I opened my eyes, I was peering at my own vomit, which lay at the bottom and sides of a plastic bag, colored the same brown as the plastic garbage can it lined.

I looked up and saw my buddy Kip doing the best he could to hold the garbage can in one hand and my head in the other, trying to keep me from choking. A nurse soon joined him. After the spasms subsided and my breathing was restored, my attention was drawn back to the pain. It was an unthinkable pain, sharp and severe, the likes of which I had never before experienced.

The white plaster cast started at my toes, continued up past my knee, and then disappeared under the covers. I reached down to feel. It was all the way up to my ass. Realization suddenly replaced my confusion, and I started to wail, tears running down my cheeks.

"I was supposed to get scoped, that's all, Kip. What the hell happened?"

"Oh, man, here he goes again," the nurse said, as she roughly pushed me to the side, causing even more pain to course through my leg. Hurriedly she threw the covers aside, jabbed a hypodermic needle into my butt, and pushed the plunger down. The morphine's effect was immediate, and a level of calmness overtook me as I pulled the covers back over me, gently floating back to my prone position on the bed.

"What's her problem?" I asked, as she left the room, silently muttering to herself.

"I guess you don't remember, huh?" Kip asked, grinning.

Over his shoulder, I noticed through the window that it was night, the city lights stretching out and then stopping abruptly at the Detroit River.

"It's dark out. What time is it?"

"You've been out all day, man. It's nearly 9:00 at night."

Kip proceeded to fill me in on the events of the day.

"Tiege was in here to see you three times, hoping to catch you awake so he could explain the situation in person. In fact, he was just here a few minutes ago."

"Did he tell you what happened?"

"Yeah, he explained everything to me. He wanted to be sure I knew all the details, so I could tell you everything in case he wasn't here."

"He said as soon as they put you out he tested the knee. With your muscles relaxed, he knew right away your ligament was wasted. He said your knee just bowed right out, like this." He demonstrated with his hands, sending a chill up my spine.

"The medial collateral ligament?"

"I think that's what he called it. It's the one that runs along here." He motioned with his finger along my cast, drawing a line from the bottom to the top of the inside of my knee.

"Anyway, the ligament pulled completely away from the femur, where it attaches up here." He again showed me where he meant, pointing to a spot on my cast above and inside of the kneecap.

"He attached it back to the bone with a washer and screw."

"They did all this through a scope?"

"No, no. They scoped you first to confirm the damage and then sliced you open. You've just had major knee surgery. They had to put you out for a long time. Whatever they did took a lot longer than they had first anticipated. But for whatever it's worth, Tiege said that if you're going to blow out your knee, this is the best way to do it. He said the repair was clean, the ligament was in good shape, and your knee should be as good as new."

"Yeah, that sounds like Tiege. I guess I won't be playing next week, huh?"

Kip didn't bother answering the question, knowing I certainly had to know the answer to that one.

"Do you remember anything at all from earlier?" Kip asked. The big grin started at the corners of his mouth, then spread over his entire face.

"Man, the last thing I remember I was lying on the operating table. That was what—15 hours ago?"

"So you don't remember the 'Nurse Ratched' incident?"

"You mean Nurse Ratched from *One Flew Over the Cuckoo's Nest*?"

"Yeah, you were pretty upset when you first woke up, or when I *thought* you woke up, I guess. It was a couple of hours ago. You were screaming bloody murder. You know the nurse that was just here? You kept calling her Nurse Ratched. I don't think she appreciated it either. She's obviously still pissed, the way she just stormed in here a few minutes ago. I can't say I blame her, though; you were a real asshole."

"Hey, wait a second. I don't remember any of that. How can I be a real asshole if I don't even remember doing it?"

Both of us started laughing.

"And, Dorn, you've got some crazy-ass friends, man. They showed me things last night . . . well, let's just say that you've got some crazy-ass friends!"

I started laughing even harder.

"And that's not all." Kip was laughing, too, barely able to continue his story. "Just a couple of hours ago. I can't believe I'm even joking about this; I mean, I was almost killed," he explained as he tried to catch his breath.

"I'm here all day, right, hungover because of those crazy bastards that you call your teammates, and I'm starving. So I walk down to the McDonald's on the corner. No big deal. I mean, it's still light out, and we're in the middle of Detroit, right? What's the worst that could happen? I'm sitting there, with my Big Mac and fries, and all of a sudden in walk these three big dudes with pipes, steel pipes, man, and they start whaling on this poor guy in the corner. No conversation, no trash-talking, they just come in and start whaling away! Right there in the freakin' McDonald's restaurant."

I couldn't help myself. I'm not sure if it was because of the morphine, the events of the last two days, or the way Kip was telling the story, but I couldn't stop laughing. As he continued, big belly laughs overcame me, my spastic movements causing me to hold my leg in pain.

"So I'm sitting there, starving to death, and this poor guy is getting his head beat in, and I say to myself: 'Kip, fuck the Big Mac, fuck the fries.' I left my food sitting on the table and ran out of there as fast as I could."

By the time he had finished his story, my belly laughs had subsided, and I had fallen fast asleep.

I was fortunate to have Kip visiting me that weekend to help me out (and keep me entertained) and to have Tweety and his assistant, Joe Recknagel, to supervise my rehabilitation. However, I was most fortunate of all to have Dr. Tiege perform my surgery and oversee my recovery. I couldn't have had a better surgeon and doctor, and he couldn't have had a better patient.

Armed with cutting-edge technology, the latest rehabilitation techniques, and a very motivated 22-year-old, Tiege set up a schedule that had me back on the field in an unprecedented seven weeks. I'm not sure if that was a record at the time, or if possibly it still is a record, but there aren't many people who have played in an NFL game seven weeks after having major knee surgery. That's the good news.

The bad news is that during my hiatus, we won only one game, our downward spiral at least partially fueled by that idiotic "Another One Bites the Dust" parody a few of my teammates recorded right around the time of my injury. Their own lyrics replaced the original words, written by John Deacon and sung by rock icon Freddie Mercury and the legendary band Queen, but the chorus—*Bamp, bamp, bamp. Another one bites the dust!*—was kept intact. The cocky, self-serving lyrics, cowritten and sung by Jimmy "Spiderman" Allen, a defensive back, lauded the superiority of the Lions, highlighted the incredible attributes of himself and a few other select teammates, and hailed us as the eventual Super Bowl champions. That song, along with an accompanying video, was quite popular while we were winning but served as an example of what selfishness and greed can do to a team when we were losing. It certainly contributed to our eventual demise, and was turned against us when the losses started to pile up.

That stupid song was rubbed into our faces time and time again and was played by our opponent's band after every away loss we suffered for years to come. How humiliating it was to hear *Bamp, bamp, bamp. Another one bites the dust!* as we walked off the field after a loss. I am just now able to listen to the original song, actually a great tune, without feeling nauseated.

Protected by a larger, more beefed-up version of an Anderson Knee Brace, which currently is standard equipment on both legs of most interior linemen, I played hard those last three games of the year. We won all of them but just missed the playoffs with a 9–7 record.

Surgery became rather routine for me after that. I stayed healthy the whole next year, but the washer and screw used to affix my medial collateral ligament had really started to bother me. The constant friction was causing swelling and discomfort, and it was decided that as soon as the season was over they'd remove them.

I was also having trouble with my right ankle. My left ankle, which I had sprained when I blew out my knee the year before, had healed without any problem. It was the other one that was giving me problems, the one I had sprained countless times, and it had become permanently swollen. It was decided that while they had me on the table and knocked out, Dr. Tiege would clean it out and do a little exploration in there to see what was up.

The surgery was scheduled for two days after our last game. This would become routine for me, getting operated on two days after the season ended, and is when the majority of my dozen or so orthopedic operations were performed.

Dr. Tiege, the master of understatement, explained that both surgeries were very minor and once again made it sound like we were going downtown for a burger and a movie rather than for orthopedic surgery.

I again found myself doped up, scared, and alone, lying in the corridor outside of the operating room. When I woke up this time, Kip wasn't there and neither was "Nurse Ratched," but I was in a lot better shape than last time. However, although both surgeries were minor, both the knee and ankle were sore for weeks, and because they were on different legs, I had a real problem getting around.

Dr. Tiege said my knee looked great, but my right ankle was a different story. He had pieced together what was left of the five ligaments on the outside of the ankle, but there wasn't really that much left to work with. Needless to say, it still bothers me to this day, and when I walk or try to run, it's mostly on the outside of my heel.

The following year, again just a few days after the last game, I needed an operation on my chronically sore left shoulder. It had bothered me all season, and the cortisone shots I had received every few weeks only masked the pain and soreness. Even though my right shoulder didn't feel nearly as bad, it was decided that while they had me on the table they'd operate on that one as well, the tests showing almost as much damage to that one as the left.

You would have thought I'd have learned from the previous year. I could walk this time, but I couldn't move either arm more than a few inches from my sides for the next week, making many of life's mundane but necessary tasks, tasks you take for granted when you have use of your arms, nearly impossible.

There were many more surgeries to follow. I had several more on my left knee and operations on an elbow, thumbs, digits, two discs dissolved in my lower back, and a partridge in a pear tree. There were so many that I lost count.

The title of this chapter, "Broken Bones!," is in reference to a phrase made popular by my high school teammates Sammy Landis, Eric

Leiser, and the late Paul "Noodles" Duracinski, among others. Sore and tired after a game or practice, it was our way of communicating and commiserating with each other about our bumps and bruises. That chant, long and drawn out, with emphasis on the two *b*s, still echoes through the deep recesses of my brain: "Broken bones!"

Similar phrases abounded around the training rooms throughout my career, no matter whether it was high school, college, or pro. I guess it's just the way football players deal with those nagging, day-to-day injuries that are inherent in the game of football.

Many a time after a game, lying on the training table with ice bags affixed to various parts of my body, my Detroit Lions buddy Chris "Deets" Dieterich would come into the training room with, as usual, a big grin on his face and utter: "Keith Dorney, a man just barely alive!"

Frank Case, a good friend and teammate from my Penn State days, had all the offensive linemen calling each other "fools," as in "Hey fool, whatcha doin' after practice?" It stood for Fraternal Order of Offensive Linemen, and there were times when we felt it was a very appropriate moniker indeed.

Many times I'm asked if it was all worth it—the countless surgeries, the concussions, the *broken bones*, the endless hours of training under the hot sun. My answer is always the same. It's not the game I miss so much, and I certainly don't miss getting cut open on a yearly basis. It's the guys that made it all worthwhile. The countless cast of characters, from high school on up, that I've had the pleasure of meeting and of sharing hardship, good times, victory, and defeat. That's what I miss most about the game, and, yes, if I had to do it all over again, I'd do it in a heartbeat.

Chapter 3

The Morning After

A twangy, unfamiliar rhythm slowly made its way into my consciousness, gently nudging me from sleep. I lay there in the darkness, eyes closed, silent beneath the single sheet of linen. Suspended in the frail and usually fleeting veil between sleep and reality, my mind worked to extend this time. I didn't want to get up and face what was at hand. Maybe, just maybe, I wasn't lying in a rented bed in Lake Orion, Michigan, but in a more secure haven, one far removed from my current reality.

The image was not clear at first, but as I slipped back into dream time, the scene slowly came back into focus. There was a pond, with water so still it looked like a giant mirror. The sun was shining, but the reflection on the water was muted by the mist that clung to the water's surface. The fog continued up the slope to the orchard, where fruit hung heavily from the branches. Through the early-morning haze I could see that some of the tree limbs were supported by wooden stakes, the sign of a well-maintained orchard. Two dogs, one fully grown and one a puppy, played by a large greenhouse. Shades of green exploded from the canvas of clear glass covering it, hinting of a bounty of fresh edibles within.

A tidy barn was in the foreground, its classic lines framed by a rusted tin roof. The weather-worn redwood siding blended in perfectly with the colors around it—the soft browns of the native grasses, the border fence, the gravel driveway, the collective greenish-brown hue of the forest beyond.

Past the pond, rising up out of the mist, was a large hill. Oak, mandrone, and douglas fir rose majestically from the north-facing slope, forming a seemingly impenetrable canopy. Tufts of mist still hung over some of the taller branches. Beams of sunlight made their way through the mist, giving the scene a surreal quality.

The brilliant blue sky, the freshness of the marine-tinged air—I could smell it! It seemed so real. Could it really be true? Was I waking up into this dream? Was this reality? I wished it so. I clung to it desperately.

The song emanating from the tiny clock radio by my bed droned on. Maybe during the night I was somehow magically transported to this place and was living the way I always thought I should be living, even though I had no idea where that might be. A man's voice replaced the melody. I struggled to listen to the muffled voice of the disc jockey through the tiny one-inch speaker. Maybe he would tell me where I was. A ranch in Texas? A farm in Pennsylvania? Maybe a spread in the coastal mountains of Northern California?

I continued to listen to the disjointed voice, listening for the station's call letters, hoping to discover my whereabouts.

A slow, rhythmic slurping sound drowned out the voice on the radio. A wet sensation spread across my face. As my senses began to flicker back, I finally realized that my dog, Boss—my longtime friend and companion—was licking my face, telling me it was time to get up and let him outside. He was taking full advantage of my clouded perception, getting in more than his usual cursory licks.

The elated feeling, the picturesque images, the dream, dropped out of my brain like a rock. They were immediately replaced by feelings of dread and hopelessness. Physical pain overtook my consciousness as I attempted to sit up in the now dawn-lit room.

Looking through the two unshaded windows in front of me, I noticed the overcast, gray sky and what looked like rain clouds. Did the sun ever shine in the state of Michigan? This year seemed gloomier than the previous six autumns I had spent here. The sky and the flat landscape outside my window, the furnace-heated air, and the four blank bedroom walls were such a stark, dismal contrast to the vivid colors and images of my fast-fading dream. I wanted to go back to sleep.

I reached over and peeled back the bedsheet that had adhered itself to the underside of my left forearm during the night. It was stained a sickening brownish yellow.

"Shit," I muttered under my breath, as I raised my left elbow toward the ceiling and rotated my shoulder back to better view the contusion. Midway through this simple motion a sharp pain coursed through my shoulder.

"Fucking Christ!" I stopped and gingerly lay back down on the bed.

"You're so eloquent this morning, dear," my wife, Katherine, said sarcastically, as she rose naked from the bed to let Boss out the back door. I winced as I again, this time more cautiously, tested the tender shoulder.

I raised my forearm slowly upward and was met with a sharp, stabbing pain from deep within my shoulder before I even got my forearm parallel with the bed. I tried rotating it in a circular motion outward, away from my body, but again the pain stopped me. Rolling it inward wasn't quite so bad. I knew I would have to get another cortisone shot in that shoulder this week if I had any hope of playing next Sunday.

"Oh, honey," Katherine murmured sadly, as she examined the weeping wound on my arm. She placed a small glass of water and two large orange pills on the bedside table. She stroked my bushy, unkempt hair, smoothed my blond eyebrows back in place, and tenderly kissed me on the forehead.

"Look on the bright side, babe; there are only eight games left in the season. We can do that standing on our . . ." I started to say, as I watched her walk out of the bedroom, getting distracted by her retreating form and those long, long legs.

She stopped in the doorway and turned around to face me.

"*Only* eight games? That's not funny, Keith. Your continuing to play football when you can barely walk isn't funny either. And the fact that you can't lift either one of your arms above your head? And the only way you can play is if they stick you full of needles? Not funny! Can't you see what you're doing to your body?"

She started to leave but once again thought better of it and turned back around.

"And why the hell won't you wear some arm protection out there so your arms don't end up looking like something out of a horror movie?"

"What, the arm? It's only a flesh wound," I smiled, doing my best Monty Python impression.

"Oh, God, I'm married to a freak," she said, as she left the room for real this time, trying to suppress a smile, shaking her head as she disappeared into the bathroom. She knew I wouldn't wear arm protection. I had never worn any type of arm protection. A savvy defensive lineman could grab it, pull it to one side or the other, and gain an advantage over me on pass protection. At least that's what I claimed when asked about it. In reality, it was actually Jon Kolb's fault.

If I ever had an idol, a player I emulated, it would have had to have been Jon Kolb of the Pittsburgh Steelers, and he was the reason I would never, ever wear anything on my arms. When I was attending Penn State, I'd often watch the Steelers play on television Sunday afternoons. I grew up a Philadelphia Eagles fan, hailing from the other end of Pennsylvania, but the television stations around State College broadcast the Pittsburgh games exclusively, and most of my friends back in Jordan Hall were rabid Steelers fans.

I remember Kolb, their stalwart at left offensive tackle for many years, running up to the line, his massive arms void of any kind of pads except for a pair of lightweight boxing gloves he wore to protect his hands. He'd get down in his stance, and you could see his massive triceps muscle bulging out of his left arm. He was relentless, punishing his opponents when they ran the ball, deftly pushing his man past the pocket when they passed.

I mentioned my admiration of Jon Kolb to my brother, Craig, and he sent me Kolb's football card. I couldn't believe it. The guy, at least in that particular picture, was a dead ringer for me.

From that moment on, I was a Jon Kolb wanna-be. I played in Pittsburgh during a blizzard and subzero temperatures, in Green Bay when the wind chill was ⁻40 degrees, and on the rock-hard, extremely abrasive AstroTurf surfaces of the Pontiac Silverdome and Veteran's Stadium in Philadelphia. I never, ever, wore anything on my arms.

Back to the wound on my forearm. It was quite a nasty one. It was wider at the top near the elbow, about 4 inches across, and tapered slightly as it traveled toward the hand. Its boundary took up almost half of the surface area of my forearm. It traveled clear down to just above my wrist, a distance of nearly 10 inches.

Katherine returned with her supplies and put them down on the nightstand. As she studied the arm more closely, she grimaced. The normal hairy, winter-white skin of my forearm was nearly gone. It was replaced by what looked like bright crimson raw hamburger meat. Hundreds of tiny red bumps protruded upward, each one oozing clear fluid. The rest of it was an angry-looking red that looked like someone had taken a serrated knife and scratched it back and forth until you couldn't see the skin beneath.

The culprit in this case was not a Minnesota Viking, whom we had played the previous afternoon, but the ancient, crumbling AstroTurf that covered the arena floor of the Pontiac Silverdome. The Detroit Lions did not own the Silverdome. The city of Pontiac, Michigan, owned it, and the story went that the cash-strapped city was trying to get a few more years use out of the long-ago worn-out rug.

The "blades" of fake grass were worn, ripped, and faded. Green spray paint needed to be applied to it for the benefit of the television viewing audience. The green paint mixed with blood, sweat, snot, thrown beer, and God knows what else that was spilled or spewed on the carpet during a game, making for a rather unsanitary surface, to say the least.

Looking closer at the arm, it was actually a reflection of the turf itself. The tiny blades of fake grass were irregular, stiff, and extremely abrasive. Their imprint could actually be seen in the many bumps from which millions of my spent white corpuscles emanated.

I painfully reached for the two football-shaped 800-milligram horse pills of Motrin on the nightstand and swallowed them in one gulp, not bothering to chase them down with the water. Motrin's active ingredient, ibuprofen, was an anti-inflammatory pharmaceutical that helped relieve the painful swelling in my joints. I knew I popped far too many of the things, but at this point in my career, I would do almost anything to line up on Sunday.

Like my teammates, I had access to a nearly endless supply of them from the Lions' medical staff. As a joke one Halloween, Katherine, dressed as a "good witch," had filled a bowl with them and given them out to all the "good boys" who attended our costume party that evening.

Incredibly, I had ingested 24 of the tablets over the past weekend alone, and I knew some of my mates on the offensive line took even more. Even if you factored in my 290-plus pounds, that amount was still at least seven times the recommended amount. And this dosage was repeated week after week during the season. What effect would this abuse have on me in the long run? I didn't know, and at that point I didn't care. I figured this particular transgression was one of the more minor violations I was committing against my body.

"Lift your arm," Katherine ordered, as she tucked several towels under my forearm and began pouring hydrogen peroxide over the wound. As she poured the bubbly liquid over it, she rinsed it away with water, repeating the process over and over until she was satisfied the wound was properly cleansed.

"It's not always going to be this way, Katherine." I gently stroked her neck with my free hand as she worked on me. "I'm not going to play football forever. And we're going to have a little Dorney running around here pretty soon. That'll take our minds off football."

We had decided earlier in the year that it was time to start a family. Katherine insisted, though, that the only way she was going to let herself get pregnant was if she could have the baby in the off-season, in California. Her mom would be around to help out, and I was sure to be there as well. Ideally, Katherine calculated, conception should take place in late summer or early fall.

Even though I insisted otherwise, she was convinced that if it came down to it, I'd choose a football game over the birth of our child if our baby decided to be born on a Sunday. She wasn't willing to take that chance.

We both figured that immediately after she went off her birth control pills, voilà, we would make a baby. But it didn't work out that way. Maybe it was due to the dubious start to our efforts.

Katherine decided that August would be the perfect time for conception but had forgotten that I would be "locked up" in preseason camp for that whole month. She didn't let a little detail like that deter her, however. At 10:00 P.M. sharp, Katherine would be waiting in the parking lot in our customized Ford Econoline van, with a six-pack of beer and babies on the brain. I was more than game. However, in retrospect, there was very little liquid of any kind left in my body by this time, and my balls had been confined to a jockstrap for most of the day.

These soirees went on for a couple of weeks, until it just got too embarrassing for Katherine. She had sworn me to secrecy, but it's hard to keep any secret in camp when you're spending every waking moment with the same group of guys.

My offensive linemates, knowing full well what we were up to, had begun to cheer us as we climbed into the van. Our offensive line coach, Bill Muir, got in on the action, too, once ending our meeting 10 minutes early "in honor of the Dorneys' new baby."

"If you'd kept your big mouth shut, I'd probably be pregnant right now, big guy," she now said, laughing, referring to the whole camp scene.

She continued her work on my arm. From an old eyedropper that we'd converted to hold betadine, she dripped the dark red liquid over the wound until it was completely covered with the antibacterial agent, turning the wound a slightly darker shade of reddish brown.

"I like the idea of naked nurses," I kidded, surveying the movement of her ample breasts as she finished her chore. She flashed me an evil grin as she turned to leave, wiggling her butt seductively as she walked through the doorway.

I had no idea how I could have coped without her. At that point we had been married for three years, and she made those miserable, losing seasons somewhat tolerable. Our relationship flourished on many levels. We had common interests in books, music, and other intellectual pursuits, but raw, sexual attraction was definitely a major part of the mix. For me, at least, it was what attracted me to her in the first place. Those first few months we knew each other, we often wouldn't even go out as planned but just fall into each other's arms in the doorway of her apartment and make love for hours, stop to eat, and then continue throughout the night.

How did I, an easterner, drafted by Detroit, end up marrying a California girl in the first place? Well, given the circumstances, it's not that hard to imagine.

Professional football, at least back when I played, was a six-month-on, six-month-off proposition, especially for us "nonskilled" players. Linemen were asked to stay in shape, lift weights, and report to two three-day "minicamps." Beyond that, it was pretty much "see you at summer camp," which started sometime near the end of July.

There I was, at the end of my first professional football season, facing a six-month paid vacation. Personally, I had a great first year, starting every game. I was single, had just turned 22, and had money for the first time in my life. But as a team we were atrocious. The sportswriters were merciless, the locals hostile, so it seemed logical to get the heck out of Dodge. But where to go? I had lived near State College and Penn State the previous two years, but I already had my degree, and it seemed time to move on. I decided to go back to my hometown.

That seemed like a good plan at the time. Except, given the fact that my hometown was Macungie, Pennsylvania, it wasn't exactly the fast-lane lifestyle I was seeking. I ended up accepting an invitation from Russ Bolinger, who played guard next to me on Detroit's offensive line, to visit him out in Southern California. I loved the beach, was a certified scuba diver, and had always wanted to try my hand at surfing. It was a match made in heaven.

Shortly thereafter, my two good friends, Mark "Whitey" Oleska and Kip Vernaglia, ended up moving in with me, sharing my quest for the idyllic bachelor life. I had known Whitey my entire life, growing up a block from him back in Macungie, and we attended every grade together all the way through to Penn State. There we all were, sharing a house by the beach in San Juan Capistrano, California. Go figure.

Personally, the only thing I felt I really had to do during the off-season was lift weights for two hours a day, and I usually got that done by 10:00 A.M. Other than that, I could do whatever I wanted. I stayed in shape by playing my favorite sport, basketball, usually on the courts right on the sand at Laguna Beach or Dana Point. I surfed and swam nearly every day. I bought a 15-foot inflatable raft, powered it with a 40-horsepower engine, and dove for abalone and lobster off the coast.

And we partied hardy. Kip was working the nightclub circuit at the time, giving us access to concert tickets, parties, and lots of single women. The boys would take care of the house I bought while I was off playing football, and I would simply pick up where I left off upon my return. Needless to say, what a great, carefree time it was for all of us.

I was very content living the bachelor lifestyle, splitting my time between California and Michigan. That is, until we decided to hit happy hour late one afternoon in Costa Mesa, California.

Whitey, Kip, and I, plus Ronnie, one of a revolving door of roommates we would take in to fill up the house, were in attendance. I was leaning against the cigarette machine drinking a Heineken, grooving to George Thorogood and the Delaware Destroyers' "Bad to the Bone," when a woman, an incredibly beautiful woman, approached the machine. She barely glanced at me as she inserted some coins and then bent down to make a selection. I couldn't help but notice one of her many attributes as she did so. That particular attribute was accentuated by her cropped sweater, which revealed a bare lower back.

Not surprisingly, I was not the only admirer. The other one, however, was much more overt in his actions and completely lacking in social skills. This apparently drunken fool stumbled over and inserted several fingers down the back of her Levi's. I noticed immediately by her reaction that this was indeed an unwelcome intrusion, and I instinctively grabbed the little man's hand, twisted it upward, and informed him that his manners left something to be desired.

Although I did not feel threatened and certainly had the matter well in hand, the aforementioned Ronnie took it upon himself to come to my rescue. Out of nowhere he performed a perfect form tackle on the guy, one that would have made any of my teammates proud. I'll never forget standing there, dumbstruck, looking into my future wife's beautiful blue eyes, my arm still in the air where I had moments before held the unfortunate fool's hand. As he wrestled around on the ground with my roommate, I stood there, oblivious to the commotion at my feet, desperately trying to come up with something to say.

Katherine smartly ducked into the rest room, avoiding the ugly scene that followed, the bouncers making short work of the drunken idiot. I bought two more Heinekens and offered her one upon her return. She accepted the beer, politely thanked me and Ronnie for our "heroics," but flatly declined my invitation for her to join me. She explained she was with a group of friends from work and had to deliver the pack of cigarettes she had just bought to her coworker. Thank God I got up the nerve later to go and ask her for her phone number, and thank God she gave it to me.

During our first date, we both fell head over heels in love. Surprisingly, though, the fact that I played professional football almost blew it for me. We were having a fabulous time getting to know each other, talking about what books we had read, what new music we were into, and what local bands we had seen recently. What each of us did for a living had never even entered into the conversation. As I was about to take her home in my Ford van, she noticed the spare-tire cover attached to the back door. It had a picture of a majestic male African lion on it, and she commented on how beautiful it was and what a coincidence it was that I, too, liked lions. She waxed on and on about all the pictures of lions she had collected over the years and how the lion had been her favorite animal ever since childhood.

"Keith, what's your fascination with lions?" she asked innocuously. I told her about Penn State and the Nittany Lions and then explained that the lion was the mascot for my employer, the NFL Detroit Lions.

"What do you do there?" she asked.

"Why, I'm a player."

She stood there staring at me for a moment before we got into the van and drove to her apartment in Huntington Beach. Later, she explained to me what a miserable ride that was for her. After finally meeting a guy with whom she wanted to have a relationship, the "dipshit" goes and lies to her about what he does for a living, she recalled thinking.

Luckily, a coworker of hers was from Michigan, and a call back East to the coworker's football-crazy brother confirmed my employment.

From that moment on, we were inseparable. Except, of course, when it was time for me to head back to Motown for the season. The time we spent apart was torture for both of us, and she spent a good deal of time our first few seasons apart on an airplane, flying back and forth between California and Detroit. Soon after, we ended up marrying and have been together ever since.

As I lay there reminiscing about those carefree off-season days in California, the love of my life, and our incredible reunions at the airport, the pain of the moment—both physical and mental—brought me back to the present. My mind had already begun to return to the previous day's debacle, when the Lions, our back against the wall in a must-win situation, had gone out and "pissed straight up in the air," as head coach Darrell Rogers so eloquently put it after the game.

In a few hours, every movement I made during yesterday's 75 offensive plays would be critiqued, analyzed, dissected, and evaluated. Even though I thought I had played very well, my one major transgression, a damn bogus holding penalty, loomed large in my mind. It was the nature of my position, or any position on the team for that matter. You needed to perform flawlessly every play. You never knew which one was going to end up being crucial to the outcome of the game.

I slowly rolled my legs off the bed until I was sitting on the edge of it with my feet on the floor. I sat there, feeling the cool linoleum against the bottom of my feet. My right forearm, the "good" arm, lay across my thighs, helping to support the weight of my upper torso. My left arm was extended straight, with the flat portion of my clenched fist on the floor, so as to be out of harm's way and to further bolster the weight of my upper body.

I sat that way for a few moments, wondering how the hell I was going to get up to relieve myself. Flexing my abdominal muscles, I simultaneously began to shift my upper body weight from my left fist and right forearm to my back. Almost immediately I abandoned that idea, as a sharp pain seized me. The pain, emanating from my lower back and upper buttocks, subsided immediately as I transferred my weight back to my arms.

My back. It worried me more than any of my other injuries, even my left knee, which would eventually end my career. It wasn't that my back was going to prevent me from playing. I had played with back pain most of my football career. I was more worried about the long-term effect. What would my back feel like 20 years or so from now?

Ever since I first injured it back when I was a sophomore at Penn State, back pain was my constant companion. It had gotten progressively worse during my professional career, until the middle of my fifth season when it became unbearable. By that time, shooting pain down the back of my legs, all the way through to my toes, became commonplace, and a procedure called a myelography was ordered.

I will never forget the doctor's words: "You have the spine of a 70-year-old man." I was 27 years old. The doctor, a specialist, was not on the team payroll.

The Detroit Lions' team orthopedist, or, for that matter, any other team doctor in the league, would never utter such words. Although indisputably as a group the very best in their profession, their job was to get you back on the playing field as soon as possible. Alerting one to the degeneration of one's body certainly was not in the best interests of the team.

It didn't really matter. By that time in my career, I was a true professional with an "old-time football" mentality. All I wanted that doctor to do was figure out a way to get me back on the football field, preferably the following Sunday. And if he could make those shooting pains down my legs go away in the process, that would be a bonus.

I examined the X rays with the doctor. The myelography, which in later years would be replaced by the less invasive MRI, involved shooting a dye into the lower back and then taking pictures of the area. The dye made it easier to see the discs between the vertebrae. I remembered the images being hung from a light table mounted on the wall at eye level. The lights in the room were lowered to better illuminate the film.

All of the X rays showed my sacroiliac, the very bottom of my spine, and the five lumbar vertebrae directly adjacent. Lumbar vertebrae are numbered from top to bottom, L1 to L5, with L5 being next to the sacroiliac, around the start of the crack of your butt.

Each picture was taken from a different angle, so when viewed one after the other, it was like viewing a three-dimensional image of the spine. He showed me the many bone spurs, or "loose bodies" as he called them, floating around my spinal column.

The myelography also revealed a severely bulging disc between the fourth and fifth lumbar vertebrae. The disc was bulging, not ruptured, which made me a candidate for a relatively new procedure called a kemopapane injection. It involved taking a needle, a really, really big needle as I recall, and injecting an enzyme directly into the bad disc. The enzyme, derived from unripened papaya fruit, literally dissolved the disc from the inside, taking pressure off the sciatic nerve, which was the culprit of those damned shooting pains.

The alternative, the dreaded laminectomy, involved slicing you open, removing the disc, and six or more months of rehabilitation. After personally witnessing about a 50 percent recovery rate among my peers from laminectomy surgery, I opted for the injection.

I willingly became a shining example for this new medical technique.

The surgeon never had a better patient. The shooting pains were gone, and the X rays revealed that the disc had shrunk down to nothing. I remember expressing concern over this "disclessness" after personally reviewing the X ray. Wasn't that disc there for a reason? I was relieved to find out that I "really didn't need that." This was the team doctor talking here, of course. Over the years I discovered that you "really don't need" quite a few body parts. Things like anterior cruciate knee ligaments, chunks of cartilage from a knee or elbow, and bursa sacs were merely insignificant body parts just waiting to be ripped, severed, drained, or removed.

Although much less invasive than surgery, the body still reacted to the loss of the disc. Severe lower-back spasms raked my body for the rest of the season. These were partially relieved by hot whirlpool baths and lots and lots of Valium, which, in addition to whacking you out, acted as a powerful muscle relaxer. Luckily, I didn't have access to this drug in the off-season. Three straight months of taking Valium nearly every day had definitely caused a dependency. I certainly wouldn't have been the first player to develop a doctor-prescribed pharmaceutical habit from the NFL's little black bag.

To the surprise of no one who knew me, and to the great surprise of the back specialist who performed the procedure, I missed only three games.

My "old man's spine" still bothered me, but the shooting pain down my legs thankfully never returned. Knock on wood.

I could only laugh at myself as I sat there on the edge of the bed, unable to get up to pee. I wondered what it would be like when I truly *was* old, not just old by NFL standards. Would my many ailments heal and get better, or would they worsen? Again, I dismissed these negative thoughts from my head. As was preached to me over and over during my lengthy football career, I needed to concern myself with this week's opponent, not some far-off time in the 21st century.

With a Herculean effort, I see-sawed back and forth on my butt and finally made it to my feet.

I limped to the bathroom and relieved myself.

It was going to be a long week.

Chapter 4

Women of the Game

This chapter is dedicated to all of the football wives and football moms, those poor tortured souls who are forced to watch the ones they love go out and put their bodies at risk time and time again. Through stifling heat and humidity, driving rain, freezing cold, and even blizzards, they sit there on the rock-hard bleacher seats, hoping and praying that their man's—or boy's—luck will hold out for just one more game and that he will come home to them in one piece.

It's not easy, I've been told. What's going through the heads of these women as they sit there, watching helplessly? I can only imagine.

That's why I'm going to turn the mike over, so to speak, to the two most important women in my life, my wife and my mother. I invite you to take a firsthand peek into their world.

First, I'm going to slap you into a seat on the 50-yard line at a Detroit Lions home game, right in the middle of the players' section. I think you'll find that being a professional athlete's wife definitely has its challenges. With my wife Katherine's help, I've recounted one particular afternoon and will tell it through her, using her words, thoughts, and recollections.

Mothers may have it the worst of all. To watch the body that you brought into the world go out and purposely play the game of football is almost too much to ask. After my wife's story, I give you my mother's personal account, written in her own words, of what it's like to be a football mother and her tips on how to be a better one.

She passed away in 1994, but I'm sure she wouldn't mind me reprinting here her short memoir entitled *Football Is a Mother's*

Game. She tried, unsuccessfully, to get it published back in 1975. I'm honored to have it published here.

I think you'll find that my mom writes very well. She earned her journalism degree from my alma mater, Penn State, and worked as a reporter for the *Bethlehem Globe Times.* Although she does come off at times sounding like a June Cleaver wanna-be, please remember that it was written nearly 30 years ago, and I know for a fact she purposely wrote it at least slightly tongue in cheek.

Now, I'm turning it over to the ladies . . .

Pontiac Silverdome, Minnesota Vikings
Versus the Detroit Lions, November 9, 1986

I had a death grip on the arm of my chair and bit my bottom lip as I looked up from the cement floor in front of me to see the offensive huddle break and the Detroit Lions players jogging to the line of scrimmage. The thick, acrid cigarette smoke clinging to the rafters of the Pontiac Silverdome, the unseasonably warm October afternoon, the press of the crowd, and the tension of the moment had me on the edge of nausea.

I watched my husband Keith limp to the line of scrimmage and assume his position. He was playing hurt, again, and I wished this game was over, that it was *all* over, and he would never have to take another step on that rock-hard, AstroTurf-covered concrete floor they called a football field.

I squirmed nervously in my seat and clenched my jaw as an uneasy feeling rose in the pit of my stomach. The Detroit Lions' offense needed to score right now, on this very possession, to have any hope of pulling this thing out, and they had to do it with lousy field position. They were starting this offensive series near their own end zone.

"Come on, Lions," I hissed between my teeth, as I watched the linemen get down in their stances.

The two guys in front of me stood up on their seats and started howling their own encouragement, blocking my view of the field. They were annoying from the moment they stumbled down the aisle a few minutes earlier, terribly excited to be this close to the action after sneaking down from wherever their real seats were, probably in some nose-bleed section.

This section, on the 50-yard line directly behind the Lions' bench, was where the players' tickets were assigned, making the group a collection of mostly players' wives, like me, and/or girlfriends. I throw the "and/or" in there because a few of the players actually had both sitting right here in the same section. Keith told me of one particular teammate who had a seating chart of the players' section in his locker, and would trade tickets with other players to ensure that his wife and girl-friend (or "freak," using the vernacular of the day) would have plenty of seats separating them.

Some of the wives had small children in tow, dressed up cute as a button, sporting the latest kiddie fashion or perhaps an exact miniversion of Dad's jersey. Thrown into this mix was a sprinkling of parents, miscellaneous relatives, and friends.

To a lot of these women, choosing the right outfit for the game was seemingly the most important decision of their lives, and tremendous effort, thought, and money went into it. The results varied. There were classy thousand-dollar outfits, designer dresses, furs, and leather—always lots and lots of leather. Some looked real good; however, a few ended up looking like they belonged at a high-class bordello rather than a football game.

I admit that my first year as a "player's wife," I succumbed to the peer pressure and played this fashion game. By 1986, however, I was sitting back and enjoying my veteran wife status, content with my pretty top and a comfortable pair of blue jeans.

I left the big cleavage, skin-tight pants, and high leg shots for others.

It can be quite the sideshow at times.

Although the two hooligans seated in front of me were beyond inebriated, the fact that they were surrounded by beautiful women didn't pass them unnoticed. Their leers, cat-calls, and gestures, which they didn't even attempt to keep discreet, made them just that much more annoying.

The Lions' offense kept the ball on the ground the next few minutes, with tremendous success, running to my husband's side almost exclusively. After a few of the plays, the defensive players shoved and cussed at Keith, apparently not real happy with the fury and intensity with which he played.

As usual, but especially in the fourth quarter when the game was on the line, he went all out right up until the whistle blew, throwing his big body around with absolutely no regard at all for its well-being. His overzealousness was never very popular with the men he played against, but I knew he couldn't care less. He'd ignore their jawing and wild body language, walk back to the huddle, and do the exact same thing the next play.

Many times the opposing players would relax near the end of a play, only to have my husband fly over a pile, looking to take off their heads. Even if he was far removed from the action and the ball, he'd always be looking to hit someone and didn't stop until he heard the whistle ending the play. Some called him a cheap shot. He claimed he was just playing the game the way it was meant to be played.

I wished he would play smarter, with more regard for his body, but I knew that anything I told him fell on deaf ears. He once told me he had one speed—all out—and if he tried to tone it down some, tried to take better care of himself out there, he'd "stink up the joint" and be unemployed and on the waiver wire in no time.

Personally, I think that's a bunch of hogwash. He already was scheduled to have at least one orthopedic operation after the season ended, this time on his shoulder, and the way he was limping around out there the last few games, he'd probably need another one on his left knee. He already had that one operated on twice, along with practically every other joint in his body. It had been standard procedure every year I'd been with him. A few days after the season ended, it was down to Henry Ford Hospital for another operation. It was like he didn't care. Sitting there week after week was like watching the same train wreck over and over, and I was sick of it. He should have quit this stupid game years ago.

I rose to my feet to see over the drunken young men, laced my fingers together behind my head, and kneaded the hollow at the base of my skull with my thumbs to try and relieve the building tension. The entire crowd of more than seventy-five thousand also realized the importance of the pending play. The roar of the multitude rose up, enveloping me, sending chills up and down my spine.

The collective throng seemed distant and uninterested for most of the game but at least for now sounded like the crowds I had experienced in the past, when the Pontiac Silverdome used to really get rocking. It would get so loud you couldn't even speak to the person seated next to you. I'd take pity on the opposing team's offensive linemen, especially the tackles, who I knew couldn't possibly hear their quarterback's cadence.

The noise lessened some as Eric Hipple waved his arms up and down, calling for quiet as he started his cadence. The football-savvy crowd immediately complied. Keith, who had been peering awkwardly inward at Eric in an attempt to hear him, resumed his normal pass blocking stance. Eric seemed to bark out his signals forever, and I knew from experience that he was changing the play at the line of scrimmage—calling an audible. I checked the play clock, the little one at the end of the field that limits the amount of time an offense has to get the play off, and watched it clicking down to two, one. I gritted my teeth, then let out a sigh of relief as the center snapped the ball just as the small, square clock underneath the east-end scoreboard changed to zero.

Keith, as well as the rest of the offensive line, did a good job keeping the Vikings players away from Eric. He stepped up, pushed hard off his back foot, and looked to throw the ball as hard as he could up the field.

The collision came from his blind side—the side opposite of Keith, thank goodness—a hard, vicious shot from the Vikings' right defensive end. I reflexively looked over at Eric's wife, Jan, for an instant and almost missed the great fingertip catch by our receiver as he fell into the end zone for a touchdown.

I unclenched my hands from behind my head and raised them in the air, cheering wildly along with the rest of the Silverdome crowd.

My joy was short-lived, however. The crowd noise went from a heart-pounding roar to near silence in an instant. My heart sank when I spotted a yellow flag in the Lions' backfield. I nearly retched when I saw Keith standing nearest the flag, arguing with the backfield judge who had thrown it.

"Holding, No. 70, offense, still first down."

The dreaded words broadcast from the field microphone confirmed what I already knew. Keith single-handedly had negated a whopping 60-yard gain and a touchdown, and probably any chance of them pulling this thing out. At least, that's what he would think. I knew him too well, and this damn holding penalty was going to make life miserable for us the entire next week.

The booing started almost immediately. The crowd, supportive just a few moments before, had turned just as fast.

"Dorney, you suck!"

"Get the bum out of there!"

The two in front of me went on and on, shouting derogatory, obscenity-laced comments at Keith, oblivious to the fact that the man's wife was sitting directly behind them.

My anger rose, the frustration of all those losing seasons rising up in me, suffocating me in a blanket of hardship, pain, and misery. I felt physically ill and wondered how I was going to take any more of it.

The next three plays went nowhere. The punting unit was called to the field. Those two had continued shouting at Keith and now increased their efforts as the offense, tired and dejected, made the trek back to the sideline and the bench, which was just a few feet from our seats.

The taller one of the two stood up on his seat again to be heard more clearly.

"Hey, Dorney! I know you can hear me, Dorney, you big fat loser. You really suck, pal! Time to hang it up, fucker. Dorney, hey, Dorney! You just lost the game . . . ."

That's when I snapped.

"Shut up and go back to your *real* seats, assholes!" I blurted out, more viciously and a lot louder than I had intended. Suddenly, all eyes in the vicinity were diverted from the field and were staring directly at me.

The two turned around to find a defiant, red-faced Katherine Dorney glaring at them, leaving absolutely no doubt as to who had said it.

Apparently, I wasn't the only one who had heard enough from these idiots. Out of the corner of my eye, I saw two security guards rushing up the aisle from the field.

"Why you *fucking bitch*, who the fuck . . ." the taller of the two started to say.

"Don't you talk to me that way," I said, poking my rolled-up program in his chest, causing his half-full beer to spill on his shirt, adding to his growing rage.

He had stopped his tirade midsentence, temporarily taken aback by what he must have thought was some crazed lunatic woman with a death wish. Stepping up on his seat once again, he bounded over it to face me, pulling himself up to his full height, which was still a few inches shorter than me.

"I thought I told you and your friend to get your drunken, sorry asses *out of here!*" I screamed, not even thinking or caring about the consequences of my words. I can't ever remember being so mad.

"Who the fuck do you think you are?" he slurred, moving to just inches from my face. I'll never forget his putrid, disgusting breath and, despite my precarious predicament, I wondered for a brief moment if this guy had ever heard of dental floss.

"I've got a mind to . . ."

Just then, the faster of the two security guards arrived and grabbed the drunk roughly by the shoulder. He sealed his fate by unwisely turning and throwing a wild punch in the guard's direction.

The ensuing scuffle turned ugly. The two drunks put up quite a struggle, but the Pontiac Silverdome security staff, well versed in handling drunk, brawling patrons, made quick work of them.

Suddenly, I found myself shaking with fear, then embarrassment. Tears welled up in my eyes as I began to realize how close I had come to getting myself into some real trouble.

A hand gently took mine. There was another soft touch on my shoulder. I was guided back into my seat. My daze started to clear, and I found myself with my head in my hands.

"They were starting to piss me off, too. You did us all a favor. And that looked like a lousy call against Keith," a soft, soothing man's voice said. I looked up to see a huge, smiling middle-aged man, probably the dad of one of the players, reassuring me from a few seats over.

I nodded but said nothing. I put my head back down in my hands, still too embarrassed to look up.

"You go, girl!"

"Way to go, Katherine!"

"Don't you be messin' with Mrs. Cheese!" I heard from my girlfriends, yelling and laughing, as the two young men were hauled away up the stadium stairs.

I wanted to crawl into a hole and die.

The boos, loud and unwavering, grew with intensity the closer the Vikings got to the goal line. They kept the ball on the ground, eating up the remaining time left on the clock, the Lions' defense seemingly powerless to stop them.

The game was over. The Lions had just used their last timeout, and all the Vikings offense had to do was snap the ball and take a knee for a few plays. Even though the stadium was now half empty, the boos seemed to intensify, the remaining patrons more than making up for their departed brethren.

I barely looked up from my hands. The game, the booing, and the events of the last few minutes had drained the life out of me. It seemed the more games I watched Keith play, the more I was becoming like him. I was taking this loss almost as hard as he surely would and had made a complete ass out of myself in the process. I wanted out. At that moment, I wanted Keith and me to get as far away from the Pontiac Silverdome as we could, leaving this debacle they call a football season behind, never to return.

The players' reception area, if you could even call it that, was a blacktopped truck ramp that ran from the field to a big metal entry door leading to the parking lot. The big metal door, which was just large enough for an 18-wheel tractor trailer, was flanked by two regular-sized entry doors on either side.

These doors, as well as all the doors in the Silverdome, were kept closed because the dome's massive fabric roof was partially air-supported. Whenever someone entered or exited the tunnel through one of the smaller entry doors, which was almost constantly, a strong blast of outside air rushed in, streaming through the tunnel until finding equilibrium at the field entrance.

The earlier truck traffic had left the blacktop filthy. Small particles of dust, cinders, and dirt blew up into the air whenever a door was opened, wreaking havoc among us. It was a dirty, dismal place for us to await our fallen warriors.

Yet another gust of wind blew in, blowing up the dress of the woman standing next to me, exposing her legs and backside. She was a pretty young thing, and she let out a little shriek before quickly smoothing down her knee-length red silk dress. She giggled along with her girlfriends. I couldn't help but wonder for whom they were waiting.

Despite the wind, dirt, and smoke, the group smelled heavily of perfume.

I fell into conversation with a potpourri of players' wives, parents, and siblings, settling in for the long haul, knowing that Keith, as usual, would be one of the last players out of the locker room. Why he took so long was a mystery, but after attending every home game the last two years, I had gotten used to it and accepted it as just the way it was with him.

The conversation turned inane, boring, and uninteresting, more talk about money, clothes, and football. I smiled and tried to look interested.

Suddenly, everyone simultaneously stopped talking and stared directly behind me. I turned and was genuinely astounded to see my husband, sweating and grinning, standing behind me.

"What in the world? How did you get out of there so fast?" I exclaimed, throwing my arms around him.

"Let's get the hell out of here," he whispered into my ear.

I politely introduced Keith to the members of the group he didn't know, we said our good-byes, and we started to make our way through the mass of people.

"Man, I can't believe all the folks in here. There's got to be 60, 70 people," he said, as he stopped to sign an autograph for a young boy.

"Duh. You've never been out here this fast, ever. What gives?" I inquired.

He finished his autograph, smiling, and shook the boy's hand. Then he turned to me, still smiling, and gave me a deep, passionate, wonderful kiss, right there in front of everyone in the tunnel. I ignored his two-day stubble, which felt like sandpaper raking across my face, and kissed him back with all the enthusiasm I could muster.

I was distracted. I wanted to share my harrowing experience with him, but I couldn't help but wonder why he was out here so fast and why he wasn't acting racked with guilt over his holding penalty. He was acting so . . . normal. Something was wrong.

We wove through the crowd, nodding politely to those we passed. Keith was limping badly. I knew he'd had to get his left knee drained again before the game. Last night it was as swollen as I had ever seen it.

Keith stopped to sign another autograph.

"Honey, how is your knee? It looks like you're not doing so good."

"One hundred and twenty milliliters. A new record," he replied, still smiling, referring to the amount of liquid they had sucked out of his knee with a syringe before the game.

Sick bastard, I thought, as I watched him joking with the kid, which was way out of character for him after a tough loss like this one.

If only I could lead him out of here, get in the van and just keep driving, I fantasized. *Can't he see what this damn game is doing to him?*

After finishing with the boy, he put his arm around my waist, put his lips close to my ear, and whispered, "Katherine, I love you so much." He had tears in his eyes as he pulled away from me. I was deeply touched but still couldn't shake the feeling that something wasn't quite right. Then he said it.

"Katherine, I'm through with football. I'm serious this time. I've had it with the needles, with this jacked coaching staff, with these fans, with everything. I'm through, baby. After this season, it's all going to be over. Let's get the hell out of here and celebrate."

I led him through the airlock, out into the cool late-afternoon air, and helped him up the truck ramp to the parking lot the best I could.

"So that was it," I said to myself.

I had heard this "quitting" speech before. The first time he laid it on me was the previous year, right around the time it was apparent the Lions were destined for yet another dismal, losing season. I had taken him seriously, only to be bitterly disappointed later. He had repeated the same speech to me several times since then, with the same heartfelt emotion and earnestness he had just demonstrated. Who was he bullshitting? He wasn't going to quit. He'd forget all about this little episode in a few days and act like it never happened.

It was pathetic. He had taken to telling himself this little lie, I imagined, to help him deal with bitter defeat after bitter defeat. And, to get him through another night of pain. And, I suppose, to try and placate me.

I'm sure it hurt when they stuck those needles in him before the game, but I knew the aftermath was much worse. He would pay for his indiscretions tenfold tonight and tomorrow morning.

As we neared the top of the ramp, I looked over at him.

He smiled back at me, but I could see him grimacing in pain with every step.

"That holding penalty they called on me was such bulllshit. I didn't need to hold that guy to block him. I'm not even going to worry about it. I'll be vindicated when they see the film. So, where do you feel like eating? How about the *Fox and Hound*? We'll have champagne and really celebrate."

I forced a smile back at him. At that moment, I decided the hell with it. Good times during a miserable, losing season such as this one were few and far between. I was going to run with his sick farce and enjoy it while it lasted.

"That sounds great, honey," I answered.

He wasn't fooling anybody.

Football Is a Mother's Game, by Audrey Dorney

"That play was a belly left," I smugly told the lady sitting next to me. We were watching a local high school football game in which my younger son was playing.

I became a football mother when our older son played for the same team seven years ago, and with that experience to fortify me, I have adjusted fairly well to this most difficult role. All mothers of sons, and even grandmothers of grandsons, are potential "football mothers." From the time a boy is born, most fathers begin dreaming of their sons' athletic careers, and football usually is a part of this vision. Our older son, now married, went shopping for a little football on the day his son was born. When our grandson began walking and balancing himself with certain arm movements, his daddy exclaimed, "Look at that straight arm!" and "Doesn't he move like a tackle?" There are many similar clues that point out that football is beginning to make its appearance, and if a mother prepares herself well for the coming gridiron years, she will not have to resign herself to disgusted looks and snickers from the males of the family.

A mother first should accept her football duties cheerfully. She must expect to be on call at all hours to wash muddy, grimy T-shirts, long underwear, practice pants, knee pads, arm pads, hand pads, jockstraps, and socks. The usual time for laundering these articles is 8:00 P.M., since practice ends around 6:30, and dinner finally is served at 7:00. These essential items of equipment must be clean, dry, and ready for the gym bag each school morning. Another duty is the rather tricky process of waiting for an after-practice phone call, which the football player makes without using a dime in the pay phone. When this call is answered, the party on the other end can barely be heard saying, "Pick me up," but an experienced football mother will hear this plea and dash for the car. Naturally, she is expected to attend all games, home and away, unless bedridden with a 103-degree fever or a broken leg. Sleet, snow, wind, rain, or bitter cold weather are not acceptable as excuses for reneging from this duty.

Keeping the refrigerator and freezer well stocked is one of the most important obligations in a football mother's career. This thoughtfulness also helps to prevent irritability on the part of the practice-weary football player. An analysis of the amount of food consumed by a player on any given day reveals a typical menu of orange juice, cereal, eggs, vitamins, two school lunches, several à la carte items, at least two helpings of a full-course dinner, and a mid-evening snack of pie, milk, and a large apple. This often is topped off with a weight-gaining powdered drink that is mixed in a blender with scoops of ice cream, milk, a banana, a raw egg, and vanilla flavoring.

These required duties can become almost joyful experiences if the mother can capture the intense, almost fierce feeling for the pigskin game that seems to consume the entire male being as soon as the swimming pools close on Labor Day. This feeling cannot be attained without some knowledge of the game, and a smart football mother will begin her preparations as soon as her son starts practicing for the fall season. An encyclopedia will provide the essential facts about the field, the players, and the rules of the game. Memorizing some of these pertinent facts and then casually mentioning them when the family is listening should score a few points for the mother. After all, how many men can state that the playing field is 360 feet by 160 feet, that the crossbar on the goal post is 10 feet from the ground, or that a football weighs 14 to 15 ounces? Some evening at the dinner table, a remark such as "Did you know that the origin of football can be traced back to the ancient Greeks and Romans?" certainly should raise some eyebrows. Other facts about kickoffs, fumbles, downs, scoring plays, and team lineups will arm the reader with basic football knowledge and prepare her for the next, more difficult assignment.

This next phase of the football mother's training program involves a surreptitious study of her son's play sheets. All coaches hand out these mimeographed forms at the beginning of a practice season. The sheets explain all the plays used by the team and show the defensive lineups (when the team doesn't have the ball). When first glancing at these play sheets, a mother may be tempted to give up the whole idea and go back to reading cookbooks, but after calmly studying the hieroglyphics on the paper and recalling her encyclopedia facts, she will begin to understand the tangled lines and circles that make up different lineups and will familiarize herself with football terminology. Actually, the names of plays are fun to say—dig left, dig counter, blast counter, belly option, sweep left, belly pitch right—and how about a belly left, bootleg pass right! A defensive play sheet might go something like this: "50 Regular (cover 4 & 5, use inside outside when needed); Strong Set—go cover 1; or 65 Goal Line (also T's in and T's and E's in), cover 5." Understanding these lineups probably will be a critical test, but with a little explanation from the athlete of the family, this part of the football course can be handled, too. In reality, it is not much different than interpreting a knitting pattern: "knit 1, purl 2, slip stitch, knit 1, pass slipped stitch over, knit two."

Now, the duties are organized, the facts and mechanisms of football are understood, at least better than before, but a mother still is not ready to enjoy the thrills of an actual football season until she evaluates and disciplines her emotions. Too many mothers, partly because of the fear of possible physical injury to their boys and partly because of pride in their sons' courageous participation in the game, say and do the wrong things at the wrong time. Emotional etiquette should initiate when a boy comes home from his first practice. He will be tired and hungry and will not always want to talk about football as soon as he steps indoors or narrate what the coach had to say that day. A mother will get sullen looks and sighs if she persists in prodding him. Amazing results develop when questions are left unasked. The boy, in his own good time, will offer details eagerly.

Watching a practice for a short time some afternoon will show any observer how much physical energy really is expended on the field. Warm-up exercises begin the session, dummies are hit and tackled again and again, and plays are run numerous times. Sometimes laps around the field are added as punishment for poor performance.

Another emotional upheaval results when a mother passes her son and his teammates on the field before a game and calls out a greeting or makes some funny remark. He will be teased by his friends, embarrassed in front of his coach, and probably tell the parent never to do it again.

By far, the biggest emotional impact on a mother is to see her son lying on the field during a game while his teammates are scrambling to their feet after a play. The impulse to scream, cry, or run to the field is almost irrepressible, but it *must* be repressed. Fortunately, most of the time, a boy is merely winded or perhaps suffering from a temporary cramp or pain from a hit he received.

I recall vividly one such emotional moment during a game when my son was injured. I sat quietly in my seat after the incident but squeezed my husband's knee continually while our son lay there on the field. Even when my husband went down to the field to find out how our son was feeling, I waited in the stands patiently. I talked with two gentlemen fans whom I knew, hoping for some words of encouragement. Later, when the coach decided that it was best that our son went to the hospital for head X rays, I walked from the stands steadily but found that breathing was a bit difficult. My husband went with our son in the ambulance, and I headed for our car in the parking lot. This was when I faltered the most. I could not find the car for a solid 10 minutes! The day turned out well, with no serious injury to our son, and we even found out at the hospital that our team had won the game. Later in the week, another football mother told me how much she admired my calmness during that game, and I half-jokingly told her that it was mostly paralyzed fear.

I think back to that episode often and know that a mother's conscientious effort to control emotions is essential if she wants to enjoy being part of a football-oriented family. Further, if she can approach her duties with a bit of humor and learn something about this fascinating All-American sport, she will be able to share an exciting part of the wonderful years that make up her son's youth.

I'm looking forward to football season. I might even have the opportunity to exclaim to someone at a game, "Wasn't that a well-executed middle trap?"

Chapter 5

JoePa

"Some guy from Penn State named *Torgonettio* is here to watch you practice today," my line coach informed me as I strapped on my shoulder pads. Those words were the start of my contact with Penn State University and with a man who would change my life forever. For the better, I now realize, although there was a time I wished I had never heard the name Joe Paterno.

It was September of 1974. I was a 16-year-old senior, sitting there in the Emmaus High School locker room with my teammates before practice. ZZ Top's "La Grange" was playing on the turntable in the corner, the volume blaring a little too loud for the capacity of the two speakers, which were perched precariously atop a row of lockers along the wall. I will forever associate that song with that day, that moment, and whenever I hear it, I can still feel the cool breeze on the back of my neck, blowing through the open locker room windows.

Yeah, they got a lot of nice girls . . . .

"Say, Penn State? They play some football up there, don't they now?" stated teammate Sammy Landis in his heavy Pennsylvania Dutch accent.

"Yeah, they do," I replied, wondering why the sudden attraction. Were they getting desperate? I was being pursued by other colleges but hadn't heard a thing from Penn State and had figured they just weren't interested.

Just let me know, if you want to go . . . .

The man who came to see me practice that day was actually named Sever *Toretti*, the head recruiter for the Penn State football program. I practiced hard that day and hoped the sharp-dressed man in the black fedora and navy blue peacoat liked what he saw.

As I walked off the practice field with my teammates, he motioned me over to join him on a bench by the tennis courts. My teammates hooted and hollered at us as they walked by on their way back to the locker room. He smiled broadly, laughing, which put me at least somewhat at ease.

He told me that I had the makings of a fine football player and that Penn State had been keeping tabs on me for several years now. He stressed that just because I hadn't heard from them until now—it was halfway through the football season—it hadn't been because Penn State wasn't interested in me. He explained Joe Paterno's policy of waiting until a player's senior high school season before making any personal contact, a practice eventually adopted as a rule by the NCAA.

He wished me luck the rest of the year and told me there was a good chance Penn State would offer me a football scholarship at the conclusion of the season.

"You won't hear from me again until all your games are over and done with," he explained. "I want you to concentrate on football and your studies. We'll make arrangements for you to come visit us up at our campus once your football season is over."

Little did I know that this meeting would put me on a collision course with a man who, in four short years, would have more influence on me than anyone ever has in my life, except for my parents.

To this day, the mere mention of that name—Joe Paterno—still sends shivers up and down my spine.

The man has the most dynamic and domineering personality of anybody I have ever met. He is intelligent and well read and possesses an amazing penchant for remembering names, faces, and facts.

I'm still scared to death of the man. Why? Because he has seemingly superhuman powers. He can see through your exterior, stare past any phony persona, and *peer into your soul* to see the real you. He's like an Italian Santa Claus with coke-bottle glasses, flood-length pants, and white socks—he knows if you've been naughty or nice. There's no fooling Joe Paterno.

My wife, Katherine, who was my girlfriend at the time, couldn't believe that the nice man she met for the first time at Penn State in the spring of 1983 was the same Joe that I had described. She was impressed with how he not only remembered my parents' and siblings' names but remembered details concerning their lives as well, eagerly inquiring about them as we chatted for several minutes. She was even more impressed when we visited the next time, *four years later*, and Joe picked her out of a crowd and not only remembered her name but inquired about details they had discussed four years prior.

When I began writing this chapter, my laptop mysteriously started crashing. Had I just written something of which Joe might not approve? Had he telepathically disrupted the electromagnetic field of my computer? It actually crossed my mind. JoePa is one *powerful* dude.

Later in that last year of high school, just after the football season ended, I arrived home from basketball practice to find Joe Paterno drinking scotch with my dad in our living room.

My mom was not only a Penn State graduate but also, like a good many people in and around Pennsylvania, a rabid Nittany Lions football fan. She was in the kitchen pinching herself when I came in through the back door.

"Keith, Joe Paterno is in our living room!"

I looked through the partition into the other room and saw him sitting there on our sofa, amiably chatting with my dad like they were old friends. He was rather smallish, and his black framed eyeglasses made him look more like an English professor than a football coach. I shrugged my shoulders and looked in the refrigerator for a cold drink.

"He's been here for over an hour. Get in there and introduce yourself!"

Now, I'm no mind reader, but at that moment I had a feeling I knew where my mom wanted me to go to school.

My nonchalant demeanor toward having a living legend in my house had more to do with naïveté than arrogance. Sure, I knew who Joe Paterno was, but I had never even been to a professional football game, much less a college one. At the time, I was more of a sports participant than a sports fan.

Plus, I was just a kid—I had just turned 17.

I remember Joe telling me that night that this was the first time he had ever visited my hometown of Macungie, a speck of a town on rural Route 100 with nary a stoplight.

That's a shocker, I recall sarcastically thinking to myself.

He told me I had quick feet for a boy my size.

"Thanks, Coach Paterno," I replied, wondering what having "quick feet" actually meant.

"Keith, my name is Joe, not Coach."

It seemed inappropriate to call him Joe, and I made a point of not addressing him by name the rest of the evening. But we did talk. We talked about all kinds of things—my basketball season, my brother and sister, my dog, even the legend surrounding the "Nittany" in Nittany Lions. Football was barely even mentioned. I ended up gabbing away with him like he was some favorite uncle.

He seemed like such a nice man, unlike the horror stories I had read or heard about other football coaches. When he left, I was pretty sure I knew where I was going to college.

Penn State used a rather soft-sell approach with me, as I later learned they did with all of their recruits. The same couldn't be said for the other schools that wanted me to play football for them.

I once had four recruiters from different schools at one of my basketball games. My poor mom was beside herself, trying to placate all of them and at the same time watch me play. Lou Holtz came and ate lunch with me and my friends in my high school cafeteria, entertaining us with some pretty impressive magic tricks. Woody Hayes sent me an autographed picture of himself, which I thought was rather odd. Bobby Bowden called several times during the year, "just to see how I was doing."

But none were more hard-core than Jed Hughes, the recruiter from the University of Michigan. He made a habit of showing up right around dinner time, taking advantage of my mom's good nature, and several times even got himself invited to stay overnight. His strategy was to get as close as he could to me and my parents in the time allotted, so when the time came for me to make a decision, I wouldn't be able to say no to him.

I was surprised Michigan even offered me a scholarship, after my less-than-impressive performance during my visit there. They paired me up with a senior defensive tackle as my host for the weekend, who I was told had quite the reputation as a "party guy." He lived up to that billing and more, and I unfortunately played right along. I think the only reason they still wanted me after that weekend was because they unjustly blamed the whole thing on him.

Ann Arbor, Michigan, in 1975 was a wild place, to say the least, and I got my barely 17-year-old butt in a heap of trouble. After watching the start of a Doobie Brothers concert, we went to catch the last two periods of the Michigan/Michigan State hockey game. To this day, I have never witnessed a spectacle like that hockey game, if you could even call it a hockey game.

From the minute we took our front-row seats, right next to the glass, there was one fight after another. Now, I know the two schools have quite a rivalry going, but this was ridiculous. Not much hockey ever got played, and I can't even remember who won. I don't think many of the Michigan hockey players knew who won either from the looks of them when we arrived at their postgame party.

A libation I had never even heard of called tequila was being liberally passed around that evening. The hockey players, every single one of them with several stitched cuts adorning their faces from their three-hour-plus bare-knuckle brawl, were friendly, gracious, and quite inebriated hosts, and they soon adopted the "big kid" as one of their own. My experience with drinking at that point was nothing more than a beer or two, and I figured a few sips of this seemingly innocuous liquid certainly couldn't hurt too much. Before long, I was having *way* too much fun, and my host dragged a very happy me back to my hotel room.

When the knock came on my door at 7:00 the next morning, I was no longer happy. I let Jed Hughes in, I got dressed, and we went to our previously agreed-upon early morning workout. I tried not to let him know that my head was ready to split open. Midway through my workout, it was evident to Jed I was not my normal energetic self. After I hurled chunks out the back door of the weight room, his worst suspicions were realized.

"You had better get a shower and get your act together before you meet with Bo in a half hour," Jed scolded me, referring to my upcoming meeting with legendary head coach Bo Schembechler. I did what I was told, I had my meeting, and they surprisingly blew the whole incident off, never again even mentioning it.

Jed was back in Pennsylvania the next week, hounding me and my parents harder than ever.

Penn State, however, kept their distance and actually encouraged me to take a look at other schools, confident that their program would hold up under comparison.

The weekend before Christmas, my parents and I drove the three hours west to the Penn State campus. Penn State was the only school I visited that had also invited along my parents. Sophomore linebacker Kurt Allerman, who coincidentally would also end up as a teammate of mine with the Detroit Lions, was set up as my host.

I watched the team practice for their upcoming Cotton Bowl game against Baylor. Afterward, Dick Anderson, who was to be one of my offensive line coaches, gave me a tour of the library. Penn State was the only school that showed me their library.

Matt Millen as a Raider. I've known Matt for a long time, since before he joined me as my teammate at Penn State. We used to play against each other in high school—on Thanksgiving Day, no less—dating way back to 1972.

Al "Bubba" Baker was, in my opinion, one of the best pass rushers of all time during his prime years. He was also quite a free spirit and a lot of fun to be around. *Photo courtesy of George Gellatly.*

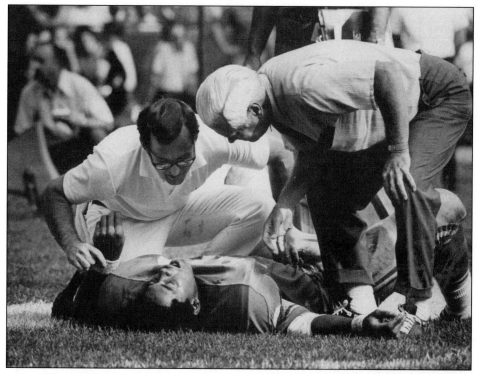

Kent "Tweety" Falb (left) tending to a fallen Charlie Sanders. Tweety has seen more head trauma, broken bones, and ripped-up knees than most emergency room doctors. *Photo courtesy of George Gellatly.*

Posing in a place where I spent a lot of time: the Detroit Lions weight room. I felt at home in its dark, dirty confines deep in the bowels of the Silverdome. *Photo courtesy of the* Detroit Free Press.

At nearly 300 pounds, I was one of the biggest players in the league at the time. My on-again, off-again beard—a backlash from Penn State's strict grooming policy—helped hide my big baby face. *Photo courtesy of the* Detroit Free Press.

Dave Pureifory. Tough—very tough. Not many people messed with "Low Rider." *Photo courtesy of George Gellatly.*

My line mate, offensive guard Russ Bolinger, talks things over with the Detroit Lions' all-important orthopedic surgeon, Robert Tiege. I shared many an adventure with both of them—on the football field with Russ and in the operating room with Dr. Tiege. *Photo courtesy of George Gellatly.*

Monte Clark prowling the sidelines. Monte, at 6'7" with size 17 EEE feet, didn't sneak up on anybody. He was not only the best pro coach I ever had, but my favorite as well.

From left: Billy Sims, an unknown hula girl, Doug English, Dallas
Cowboys head coach Tom Landry, and me at the 1983 Pro Bowl in
Honolulu.

Me and my 10-day-old son Clayton back in 1988. My wife, the photographer, is quite the artist.

Me and daughter Alea taking a dip.

Kurt took me to a steak dinner at the Nittany Lion Inn with Paterno and the other recruits. I once again made the mistake of calling him "Coach," and in return he addressed me as "Player," again telling me his name was Joe. I noticed none of his players called him Joe, at least not to his face, so I once again avoided the matter entirely, not bothering to use his name the few times I did address him.

During my four years at Penn State, I never did know what to call him and ended up most times employing this same strategy. My teammates and I, however, made up much more colorful names for him, which of course we used exclusively behind his back.

I ended up choosing Penn State for three major reasons.

First, I knew I would get a good education. I was not disappointed. As a freshman, I was required to report to the library four nights a week for three hours, where, under the watchful eye of a graduate assistant, I was required to study. If I wasn't studying, I had to *look* like I was studying. There were no paid-off professors or lackeys to take exams for me. If a player couldn't cut it academically, he was off the team and lost his scholarship, no matter *who* he was. There have been countless phenomenal athletes—one I knew personally was a potential Heisman Trophy winner—who never got a chance to play football for Penn State because they couldn't cut it academically.

We did have advantages over the other students, however. If any of us were having trouble or felt we needed some extra help, tutors were made available, no questions asked. But you had to make it on your own. Later, when I played in the pros, I couldn't believe that some of my teammates, all of whom attended a major university for four or five years, had earned less than 40 college credits. Most majors require a minimum of 120 credits to graduate.

The second reason I chose Penn State had to do with my own laziness. The Penn State football program, I thought, would be easier than the programs at the other schools. I had just read Gary Shaw's book *Meat on the Hoof*, which gave a particularly brutal personal account of big-time college football, and it scared me to death. Joe was going to take care of me while I was at Penn State. Besides, my mom loved him, and he was such a *nice* man.

The third reason had to do strictly with the football side of things. Unlike the other schools, Penn State was recruiting me as a defensive lineman. Most of the other schools weren't sure which side of the ball they were going to play me, and they'd waffle back and forth when I posed the question to them, but Penn State was adamant that it was going to be the defensive side. I had played both offensive and defensive tackle in high school, and defense was hands down my favorite. The fact that Penn State was projecting me as a defensive tackle sealed the deal.

Let's just say I was one for three.

That night in my living room in Macungie, Pennsylvania, was the last time Joe and I actually had any meaningful conversation for the next several years. Subsequent communications between us usually started with a resounding "Nuts, 'Dawney'!" (Joe's Brooklyn accent put a colorful slant on the pronunciation of my last name.) Whenever I get together with my old crew from the team, that same phrase, in the best "Joe" my friends can muster, fills the air repeatedly: "Nuts, 'Dawney,' you should have turned back there!" Or, "Nuts, 'Dawney,' you big baby, get me another beer!"

Three days before our first pads practice, they switched me to offensive tackle. Before we even had a single meaningful practice! Needless to say, I was disappointed.

My first practice with the team was a nightmare. Each player was assigned a particular color jersey, dependent on his designated "team." First-team offense was powder blue, second-team offense green, and on down the line to orange, which was rock bottom. I remember walking up to Joe that first practice in my orange jersey to ask him about my position change. That action elicited from him my very first "Nuts, 'Dawney'!," the first of hundreds more to follow.

The pace of the practice was incredible, the intensity level astounding. I wondered what the hell I had gotten myself into. Every drill, every group period, every action was literally planned and timed out to the second. How he could get over 100 football players in sync like he did was truly amazing. I have never encountered a team—at any level—that practiced as effectively as Penn State.

It was tough, way tougher than I could have ever imagined, but I survived. Before the start of the season I had fought my way up to a green jersey and earned a spot on several special teams. We had a good season and earned a trip to the Sugar Bowl to play against Alabama and their legendary coach, Paul "Bear" Bryant. What happened next scared me more than anything ever had in my young life.

Line coach Dick Anderson called me aside before our first Sugar Bowl practice. He told me that we were planning on running the ball almost exclusively and that I was going to be moved to tight end to help out with the run blocking. He said I had a chance of really contributing, something most freshmen at Penn State don't get a chance to do. I had just turned 18 the week before, and I would be facing All-American Leroy Cook most of the evening, in front of over seventy-five thousand people at the Louisiana Superdome in New Orleans and literally millions more on television. I was petrified.

Joe had me practice catching footballs during that whole month of practice, just in case we audibled to a passing play while I was in there. That actually happened several times, although no balls were thrown my way. Sensing that I probably didn't need any more motivation, he didn't say much to me during that month of practice, except to brand me with the nickname "Hammerhands."

Mercifully, Joe moved me to offensive center the following year, my sophomore season. He told me we would be facing several very talented players at nose tackle that year, and I had better be up to the challenge.

Center was a position I had never played before, and I struggled. On several occasions during practice, Joe, myself, and three defensive linemen would go off by ourselves and have our own little session, with the defensive linemen taking turns against me. We would go one-on-one with no break, sometimes for 20 minutes at a time. I had never worked so hard in all my life.

That year we played the Temple Owls at Franklin Field in Philadelphia, and I faced a particularly talented senior nose tackle named Joe Klecko. It was a long, tough afternoon for me. After the game, Joe patted me on the back and said, "I bet you're glad you don't have to play against him anymore." He was right; I was glad, although I did end up facing him several more times later in my career when he played for the New York Jets. However, I could tell from Joe's demeanor that he was proud of my effort, and his slightly sarcastic remark was his way of letting me know it.

Up until this time, Joe and I were on pretty good terms. The only time he directly spoke to me off the football field was to tell me to get a haircut, but my older teammates told me that was a good thing. I was doing well on the field as well as in the classroom. But then Joe started asking a little bit more from me, and that's when the trouble started.

In the fall of 1977, my junior year, Joe summoned me to his office for the very first time. I remember walking through the fallen oak leaves along the mall, a huge tree-lined passageway through the heart of campus, past Old Main and toward Rec Hall and his office, a feeling of dread in the pit of my stomach. What had I done wrong?

Joe got right to the point. He "asked" me to give up my current roommate of almost three years to room with a sophomore teammate who was having trouble in school. He thought that I would be a good influence on him, could monitor his progress, and could make sure that he got up for class. I wasn't too thrilled with the proposition but went along with it, feeling I really didn't have a choice in the matter.

My new roommate and I didn't know each other very well at the time. After feeling each other out for the first few weeks, we ended up getting along and became pretty good friends. Unfortunately for him, I was not up to the task Joe had given me. I lacked the maturity, mental toughness, and, I can see now, the leadership qualities necessary to assist him. I made up my mind I was only going to help him with his studies if he solicited it, which was never. If he didn't feel like getting up for his 8:00 A.M. class, I figured that was his business. He ended up leaving school before getting his degree. I had let Joe down. More importantly, I had failed to help a teammate, although I didn't quite see it that way at the time.

Then there was the infamous "chair affair." We were cruising along in my senior year at 4–0, ranked among the top five teams in the country, and looking real strong. I had just finished eating dinner after practice and was on my way back to my apartment in my old Plymouth Satellite. A teammate of mine flagged me down in the parking lot for a lift. He was holding two chairs from the dining room and explained that he had gotten permission to borrow the chairs for a poker game he was having in his dorm room that night. He secured the trunk lid over the chairs with some string, and he and his room-mate hopped into the car.

We didn't get far before the campus police pulled us over. My team-mate told the officer the same story he'd told me. Needless to say, he had not gotten permission, and the police took the incident rather seriously. I was exonerated from any actual crime, but that was the least of my worries. Joe blamed the whole chair affair on me, once again bringing my leadership qualities into question. I thought that was unfair. I hadn't done anything wrong!

After that, things *really* started to get ugly.

Joe began to ride me unmercifully. I couldn't do anything right. A few weeks later, we played West Virginia in Morgantown. I was the unfortunate recipient of three major penalties that afternoon: two holding calls and one call for being downfield on a screen pass. At least two of the calls were bogus (this is a typical response from offensive linemen, who are always innocent and *never* guilty of holding), but that didn't matter much to Joe. His entire 15-minute postgame rant was about me and me alone. He explained in great detail how my self-ishness could have cost us the game and a national championship, despite the fact that our offense scored 49 points that afternoon and we won the game by 28. His criticism of me was ruthless, and his scathing words hurt me far worse than any hits I had ever taken on the football field.

His browbeating culminated two days before we were to play Alabama for the national championship, once again at the Superdome in New Orleans. At our team meeting that evening, the focus again was on me. He stressed that we all needed to be leaders, not just on the football field, but off the field as well. The whole chair affair was rehashed again. Here we were, 11–0, ranked number one in the country, two days before we were all to play the biggest game of our lives, and he was chastising me again about those damn chairs!

My stare met his, this time more defiantly than ever. Enough with the chairs already. Enough with the almost constant harassment, the bullying, the unrelenting criticism of seemingly everything I said or did. After four years of my hanging on his every word, taking everything the man said literally and to heart, I was through trying to please him.

I felt betrayed, alienated, and worse—vindictive. If he told me the sky was blue, at that point I would have insisted it was purple. The name Joe Paterno no longer invoked fear and anxiety in me as it had for so many years. Now, it conjured up nothing but loathing and bitterness.

And, to make matters worse, we ended up losing to Alabama 14–7.

Luckily, I had no time to dwell on my newfound resentment of my coach, or on our terribly disappointing defeat for the national championship.

The very next afternoon, after the most disappointing loss of my football career, I was nearly three thousand miles away in San Francisco, practicing in pads for the upcoming East-West Shrine Game. Then, I went off to Alabama and the Senior Bowl. After that, between scrambling to finish up my spring semester classes so I could get my degree and interviewing and testing for NFL teams for the upcoming draft, I didn't have time to dwell on much of anything.

Over time, the valuable lessons that Joe had hammered home—as well as the ones he had attempted to convey—began to rise up through my anger and selfishness. Yes, some of the lessons were painful; however, the most valuable lessons in life are often the most painful ones. No pain, no gain.

I was young and bullheaded, maybe too much so to comprehend that last lesson. To be a truly great leader you needed to be one *all* of the time, not just on the football field. A leader not only does his own job well but influences the people around him and makes them better, too. I thought leading by example was enough. I can see clearly now that Joe wanted more from me.

So, Joe, I got your point. It just took me a few years to figure it out!

I think that's the essence of what makes Joe Paterno such a great football coach. No matter how good you think you are or how much you've achieved, he believes that you can always do more. That's one of the reasons why he's amassed more wins than any other Division I football coach ever. And, I might add, why he's had more football players leave school with their degree than any other coach as well, a fact I'm sure he's more proud of than the wins. For over 50 years (16 as an assistant coach and 36 and counting as head coach), he has asked the countless Penn State players he has coached to look deep into their souls and muster more than they ever thought possible.

What's truly exceptional is that his football record isn't even half the story. Life, schoolwork, and football all seemingly blurred together when he spoke. They were all the same to him. Lessons learned on the football field carried over into the classroom, your dealings with other students, and your life. He wasn't only concerned with winning football games; he was concerned about us as individuals. Sure, he wanted to win, but I know he cared about us succeeding in life even more.

I'm frequently asked, "What was it like to play for Joe Paterno?" I tell them that if I could, I'd go back and do it all over again. I think that's the biggest compliment I can give him.

Joe prepared me for the rigors of the NFL. He enabled me to get my degree. More importantly, he taught me valuable lessons I will have with me for the rest of my life.

So, Joe, my son has some *really* quick feet. Do you think you could consider coaching for, say, another couple of years?

Chapter 6

Three Bowls in Three Weeks

It was the first day of January 1979. I was in New Orleans, at the Louisiana Superdome, playing in the biggest football game of my life. Penn State was undefeated, untied, and rated number one in the country. Our Sugar Bowl opponent was the number two team in the country, the University of Alabama. The winner would be crowned National Champions.

Dressed entirely in white, except for the navy blue numerals on our jerseys and a single navy blue stripe down our helmets, my teammates and I had struggled mightily all day against a fine Alabama team. Neither team's offense could muster much productivity. Alabama, with legendary head coach Paul "Bear" Bryant roaming the sideline, was trying to hold onto a slim 14-7 advantage, with just over eight minutes to play in the ball game. The Crimson Tide offense, facing a third down and 5 from their own 25-yard line, called yet another option play. That's when the momentum turned in Penn State's favor.

Alabama quarterback Jeff Rutledge rolled to his left, faked to his fullback, and once again had Penn State junior defensive tackle Matt Millen in his face. Millen, who purposely was left unblocked on the play, had been pounding Rutledge all day long. That fact, along with his quicker-than-expected acceleration to the ball, caused Rutledge to hurry his pitch, and the ball bounced off his tailback's shoulder pads.

Penn State linebacker Joe Lally pounced on the ball. Penn State had the ball, and the momentum, on Alabama's 19-yard line. As I excitedly ran onto the field, I just knew we were going to win.

On our first play of the possession, Matt Suey ran it up the gut for 11 yards, and all of a sudden we had the ball first and goal on the 8-yard line. Mike Guman ran it to the 6-yard line on the next play, then Chuck Fusina hit Scott Fitzkee on a down and out, and now, with less than seven minutes to go in the ball game, we had a third down with less than a yard to go for a touchdown. Victory was within our grasp!

Unfortunately for me and my teammates, the next two plays go down in the annals of college football history as one of the greatest goal-line stances of all time. The sellout crowd of 76,824 was going crazy as I ran to the line of scrimmage and got down in my stance at my strong-side tackle position. Lucky for me, the referee stopped play—there was no way I would have been able to hear the snap count.

After the crowd settled down some and the ball was snapped, Suey ran the ball up the middle, advancing the ball to within inches of the goal line. On our fourth and final play, out of the "I" formation, Guman got the call, and Barry Krause stopped him cold. That play not only earned Krause the Most Valuable Player award for the game, but got him on the cover of *Sports Illustrated* the following week.

We still had a chance to win. Our defense that year was unbelievable, with Millen, Bruce Clark, Larry Kubin, and a host of other players who would go on to have stellar NFL careers. Sure enough, they stoned Alabama's next three offensive plays, and Alabama was forced to punt from their own 8-yard line. We were going to get the ball back, in Alabama territory, with plenty of time left to win.

But it was not to be. Unbelievably, we had 12 men on the field for the punt return, and Alabama maintained possession after we were penalized.

It was a horrible way to lose a ball game, but I had no time to dwell on it.

Less than 12 hours later, I was on an airplane bound for a place I had never been before, the Bay Area of San Francisco and the East-West Shrine Game. This would be the first of two postseason collegiate all-star games in which I would be participating the next two weeks. Even though we were in one of the party capitals of the world, New Orleans, on the first day of the year no less, I hadn't felt like doing much of anything after the game except going back to my hotel room and going to bed, the devastating loss draining all the fun out of me.

The same couldn't be said for the Alabama contingent on the airplane. Krause and Marty Lyons, an All-American defensive tackle for the Crimson Tide—players I had personally "run into" many times the day before—obviously hadn't been to bed. They both were bleary-eyed, unshaven, and disheveled-looking, but had wide grins still affixed to their tired faces. Who could blame them? They had just won the freakin' NCAA Division I National Championship and, unfortunately, I could only imagine what that must have felt like.

I was a little apprehensive about talking to them and more than a little jealous; however, both of them turned out to be great guys, and we ended up reminiscing about that memorable night for years to come whenever we saw each other—after our NFL games, at golf tournaments, or while traveling in the off-season.

We landed, were whisked off to Palo Alto, and, less than 24 hours after playing the biggest game of our lives, were practicing—in full pads—for the upcoming game.

Although we practiced hard, and there were quite a few NFL scouts in attendance when we did practice, the schedule was set by the East-West Shrine Game representatives, not the NFL. They allotted us plenty of free time and scheduled lots of activities for us to enjoy as a group.

We visited Fisherman's Wharf and fed the many sea lions that congregated at the pier. A Bay cruise was scheduled, with a live jazz band on board to entertain us. We feasted on local oysters and Dungeness crab and rode around San Francisco on the trolley cars.

One activity stood out from the rest and had a profound effect on everyone that attended. I clearly remember it to this day. It was the real reason why all of us were there. And it didn't involve football, the NFL draft, or how much money we were going to make.

My visit to the Shriners Hospital for Children in San Francisco was special. The young people I spoke with that day, I realized, were just like you and me. They, too, had ambitions and dreams. They just had a little bit more to overcome than the rest of us.

It was there that I realized that the East-West Shrine Game was much more than just the premier all-star football game in America. It was much, much more. Since 1925, the East-West Shrine Game has been raising money and awareness for the expert orthopedic and burn care services that they make available to kids, *any* kid, at no charge, through their 22 Shriners Hospitals for Children.

I learned I would be playing in the 54th East-West Shrine Game. The contest has been called "football's finest hour." After visiting the hospital, talking to the children, and finding out the game had raised millions and millions of dollars over the years for this worthiest of causes, I felt for the first time that I was playing in more than just a mere football game and that I was a part of something truly very special. I still feel that way. I'm proud to say that the game today is as popular as ever.

As I sat there at halftime of the game in the locker room of Stanford Stadium in Palo Alto, I still felt special but wished that our offense had been a bit more successful the past two quarters. We were down 17–7 to the West team, and losing two games in two weeks wasn't sitting very well with me.

The second half was a completely different ball game and was truly amazing. After recording a ridiculous -2 yards rushing in the first half, the rest of the offensive line and I started coming off the ball, and Russell Davis of the University of Michigan started running his *ass* off.

He rambled for six, count 'em, *six* rushing touchdowns and 199 yards in the second half. The few times the West team did slow us down on the ground, Rutledge, the University of Alabama quarterback who had helped beat me and my Penn State teammates just seven days earlier, would throw the ball over the middle to a tight end named Kellen Winslow. The future Hall-of-Famer had six catches for 125 yards that afternoon. We scored 49 second-half points and won the game 56–17.

The next morning, I was back on the plane. My destination was again somewhere I had never been before—Mobile, Alabama. I got out the in-flight magazine in the seat pocket and turned to a map of the United States. After a bit of searching, I found Mobile there at the bottom of Alabama, and I was surprised to see it sat right on the Gulf of Mexico.

A port city, I thought. *This is going to be a lot of fun.* I couldn't have been more wrong.

The first thing I noticed when I got off the plane was the smell. It was a strong, sweet, foreign smell, rather unpleasant, and it would be with me everywhere I went that week—on the football field, in the dining room, in my motel room. That ubiquitous odor permeated all of my clothes and was the first thing I noticed when I woke up in the morning. I found out later it emanated from the many pulp mills in and around the town.

"I wonder if we're going to get our own cars," I said to Chuck Correal, a fellow Penn State teammate who like me was making the three-bowl tour, as the shuttle bus pulled into the hotel parking lot.

"I would hope so," he answered. "Especially if they're going to put us up here, away from everything."

"We're trapped between two freeways," I added, noting the two interstates flowing on each side of us. *And this is no luxury hotel*, I thought, as I looked around.

It didn't take us long to figure out that that was the plan. There would be no cars, no tours, no free time, no fun of any kind. The only sights we saw were the interstate highways and a few side roads between our hotel and the practice facility. If I hadn't checked my map, I would have thought Mobile was landlocked, miles and miles from a body of water. I never did get to see the Gulf of Mexico that trip.

"You're not here for fun and recreation," we were told at the organizational meeting, held in one of the hotel's banquet rooms later that afternoon. The meeting was hosted by New York Jets head coach Walt Michaels, and he was all business. He explained that the week was going to be run just like they did it in NFL training camp, with two-a-day practices, film evaluation, full gear, and all-out contact.

I was still sore from the East-West Shrine Game the day before. Hell, I was still sore from the Sugar Bowl the week before that, and this certainly wasn't what I had expected.

"The best collegiate talent in the nation is assembled here," he went on to explain. "Your place in the upcoming NFL draft and, in turn, how much money you're going to make, will by and large be determined by not only your performance in next Sunday's game but how you perform in the upcoming practices."

"Every single NFL team is represented here, gentlemen, and they are going to be watching your every move out there. Every team period, every drill, every move you make is going to be filmed, just like it is in the big leagues. If you leave the field to take a piss, that probably will be captured on film, too."

Nervous laughter echoed around the large room. I looked around. There were some serious-looking dudes here. Some I recognized, others I had never seen before.

"At least there won't be much pressure on us this week," I facetiously whispered to Chuck.

"You will be coached this week by my entire New York Jets staff, and it will give you a taste of what it's going to be like playing in the NFL, where I'm sure most of you will end up. Good luck, gentlemen. Be sure and get a good night's sleep."

"You're going to need it," he added threateningly, as we all got up to leave.

I walked with Chuck back to his hotel room to hang out for a while before bed and was introduced to his roommate, Kirk Gibson. Kirk, a wide receiver from Michigan State, told us he also played baseball and had recently decided that he was going to pursue that sport rather than football.

Kirk's reputation preceded him. I had heard about his blazing speed—4.3 seconds in the 40-yard dash. Plus, he was big, I noticed, standing there in the hotel room. He was nearly as tall as I was and weighed a solid 220 pounds.

He too had played football the week before, in the Hula Bowl, which, at the time, was held the same weekend as the East-West Shrine game.

"Yeah, I was invited to both. I'm sure San Francisco was a good time, but I figured going to Hawaii might be a once-in-a-lifetime deal. Keith, I'm sure you were invited to both. How come you chose the Shrine Game?"

Chuck and I looked at each other. We hadn't realized we had a choice in the matter. Joe Paterno had just flat-out told us in what game we were going to play, and that was that. He had made the choice for us.

I told Kirk I had no regrets. I explained how the extreme Pacific coastline, the lush green coastal mountains, the city, the warm sunny days and cool nights, and especially the Shriners Hospital had made a lasting impression on me.

"Damn, Keith. Sounds like you really enjoyed yourself out there. Maybe you'll live there someday. Now let me tell you a little about Hawaii."

Kirk was quite the character. He entertained me and Chuck with his stories about the Hula Bowl and Hawaii, and we came to understand that besides looking to have a good time, this was kind of a farewell tour for him, a last hurrah to his football career.

"Well, I think you're nuts, Kirk," I explained to him. "Word has it you'll be a top five pick in the first round of the NFL draft. And football is a man's game. What do you want to go and play baseball for when you have a chance to play professional football?"

Thank God Kirk Gibson didn't listen to me. He of course went on to become one of the greatest baseball players of all time, playing for the Detroit Tigers and the Los Angeles Dodgers, winning championships and becoming a baseball legend. I recently watched a show put on by ESPN depicting the 10 greatest moments in baseball history. There was Kirk, barely able to run because of an injury, furiously pumping his arms as he rounded the bases. His game-winning home run for the Dodgers in Game 1 of the 1988 World Series against the Oakland A's truly was one of the greatest moments in all of sports.

Kirk and I ended up becoming good friends. We'd run into each other around town when we both played in Detroit. I took in a few baseball games during the off-season when the Tigers were in Anaheim to play the Angels, had a chance to meet some of Kirk's teammates, and got a glimpse of what it was like to be a baseball player on the road.

You have to remember that at that time, back in 1979, there were no organized "combines" like those that currently exist, where all the NFL football teams collectively get together with prospective draftees prior to the annual draft to administer a barrage of athletic, mental, psychological, and physical tests, and whatever else the NFL brass deems necessary for proper draft evaluation.

Instead, what existed was the meat market known as Senior Bowl Week.

I thought I was in pretty decent standing up to that point as far as the NFL draft was concerned, but I couldn't be sure. Other players, some from smaller schools who hadn't gotten that good of a look from the pro scouts, were determined to get noticed and make a name for themselves.

This made for a rather volatile situation. Nothing could have prepared me for that next day. The two-a-day practices—conducted in a circuslike atmosphere—bordered on the outrageous. Every drill, every play, and every down was an all-out war. Several heated fist-fights broke out, which seemed to be encouraged by the Jets coaching staff.

Sitting in my hotel room after that first day, I was more determined than ever to defend my draft status. If anything, I decided, I was going to enhance that standing. I resolved myself to do anything it took to accomplish just that.

That next day was quite eventful.

I was awakened at 7:00 in the morning by the sound of rush-hour traffic and that funky pulp mill smell. I rushed downstairs to have breakfast and found out there was going to be a small change in our routine. We were told to change into our "grays," the T-shirts and shorts we wore under our practice uniforms, and all of us were whisked off in a school bus to a local high school gymnasium.

The place was packed to the rafters with middle-aged men, the same contingent from our previous practices, the vast majority of whom were employees of one NFL team or another. We were ordered to strip down to just our shorts. At center court they had a scale and measuring device. We were to walk out onto the basketball court one by one, in full view of the crowd, where we were to be weighed and measured. The results were announced over a loudspeaker. We were then to walk back the same way we came. We were being put on display, like fashion models strolling down a runway, or more accurately, sides of beef at a cattle auction. Talk about meat on the hoof!

All of us were milling around in the outer room of the gymnasium, waiting for our names to be called, when Bob Golic motioned me over to the side. Like me, he was wearing the "old-school" shorts that barely covered our butts, and nothing else.

"If we're going to play the game, we might as well *play* the game," he explained to me as he grabbed a towel and held it out, palms up. I instantly knew what he meant. I grabbed the towel, adding resistance to it, and repeatedly worked his biceps muscles up and down until his arms were significantly swollen. Then he did the same for me. We were furiously doing push-ups, pumping our bodies up to their maximum size, when they called my name.

Golic and I were more than willing to play their game. It was obvious that this whole charade had more to do than just recording accurate weight and height measurements. They wanted to check out our bodies. They wanted to look at the size of our frames and at our musculature. They wanted to have an unobscured view of our near-naked bodies to better judge what they were going to get for their money.

I strutted out to center court, my muscles looking significantly larger than they had before our intense little miniworkout. As Golic passed me on my way back, we nonchalantly slapped hands. He looked huge.

When it was Golic's turn to "display his wares," he too gave them what they wanted, strutting proudly out in front of them. Golic definitely had a little showman in him, and I appreciated the little bit of extra help he gave me.

We were both willing to do practically anything to get an edge over the other players.

I first met Golic, a defensive lineman from the University of Notre Dame, on the football field in the Gator Bowl during our respective sophomore years. I was playing center, he was playing nose tackle, and we had quite the heated confrontation that evening. We met up again during the filming of *Bob Hope's All-American Variety Show* in Miami, where Bob Hope introduced the members of the First Team Associated Press All-America team on national television.

We were all standing there, in our full football gear, and were told we had the option of going to "makeup" before the filming started. Golic was quite the character and was the only player to take them up on their offer. I'll always remember him coming back into the room with a face full of pancake makeup, gyrating his hips like a super-model, cracking up our entire contingent.

After everyone's particulars were duly noted, they bused us back to the practice field, where a two-hour high-contact, full-pads practice was conducted, which of course was attended by the entire gymnasium crowd. The practice was filmed by no less than six cameras, with copies of each being distributed to all the NFL teams for later microscopic inspection.

Then came lunch, a short rest, and on to the second high-contact, full-pads practice of the day. I was participating in one of the more popular events, one-on-one pass rush. This drill had evolved during the week into its current state: a no-rules free-for-all where pretty much anything short of assault with a deadly weapon was allowed. The incentives to succeed were the tens and hundreds of thousands of dollars that were literally at stake. One wrong move and you're a second- instead of a first-round draft choice, or worse. The only things missing were the lions and the coliseum.

The crowd loved it. Literally hundreds of those middle-aged men would crowd around this drill, straining to get a good look at the show. And what a show it was.

This was where my hatred for Mark Gastineau first started. Little did I know at the time that my feud with him would last the next 10 years and that this would be just the first of many battles to come. At the time, Gastineau was an obscure prospect from a small school in Oklahoma, and I had heard he was here only because two more-promising defensive linemen had gotten hurt the week before in the East-West Shrine Game. Quite a few eyebrows were raised during the morning one-on-one pass-rush drill when he had beaten me cleanly with an upfield speed rush.

I purposefully positioned myself in line so I would be matched with him once again. I didn't know who the hell he was at the time but wanted to show the scouts I could block the son of a bitch.

Unlike the morning practice, this time I set up cleanly and quickly out of my stance. He lunged straight at me, as if to try and run me over. At the last instant before contact, he came across his body with his left arm, swatted my right shoulder pad with the palm of his left hand, but missed grabbing a handful of my jersey. At the same time, he attempted to swing his right arm over my head.

I had seen this "swim" move before and was ready for it. Just as Gastineau's right arm was directly over his head, I struck forward violently with both hands, catching him with the open palms of my hands, one in each armpit.

He was caught off guard and immediately tried to regain his balance, but it was too late. Staying low and accelerating my feet, I drove him back five yards before firmly planting him in the turf, my helmet driving into his face mask as we hit the ground.

Gastineau absorbed the blow and in very acrobatic fashion used my forward momentum to flip me over the top of him and onto my back. We both got to our feet and started exchanging blows furiously. Usually, whenever a fight breaks out in practice, it is broken up in good order. Not so during Senior Bowl Week. They let us fight on and on for what seemed like forever, and we were both exhausted when they finally pulled us apart.

I can only imagine what the scouts were writing down in their notebooks after that little fracas. "Good spirit, that Gastineau, but he needs to keep his right up." Or maybe, "Dorney has a good right hook but needs to work on his jab."

Gastineau greatly enhanced his status that week, and the New York Jets made him their second-round draft choice later that year.

I grew to hate Gastineau with a burning red-hot passion. And I know he had to feel the same way about me. It wasn't like I had anything against him personally. I had met him off the field on several occasions, and he seemed like a decent guy. He even let me wear a pair of his football pants for the Senior Bowl game that Sunday after I had ripped my only pair.

It was his style of play and his demeanor on the field that I detested. After recording a sack, or sometimes just for having a holding penalty called against his opponent, he was in the habit of raising his arms up and down, doing one of those "dig me" dances off by himself, shunning his teammates' congratulations in favor of congratulating himself. Those selfish acts, which would be met with an instant penalty and fine if performed today, made him a target for me and my teammates during our numerous encounters.

Although I abhorred those celebrations, I owe the man a huge debt of gratitude. It was my hard-nosed play against him—and the subsequent exuberant accolades given to me by Howard Cosell during a *Monday Night Football* game just days before the Pro Bowl balloting—that earned me a trip to Hawaii and an appearance in the Pro Bowl that year.

No one was happier than me at the end of the 2001 NFL football season, with the possible exception of Michael Strahan, when Brett Favre of the Green Bay Packers allowed the New York Giants player to sack him during the last regular-season football game of the year. That sack gave Strahan the record for quarterback sacks in a season, breaking Gastineau's old mark of 23 that he had set back in 1985.

I couldn't help but take satisfaction in seeing my nemesis' old record broken. Years earlier, I must admit I also enjoyed watching "Butterbean," a rotund, overweight, but highly skilled boxer, knock out Gastineau during his short and ill-fated boxing career. It looked to me that he still had problems keeping up that right.

Before the Senior Bowl game that Sunday, I asked Kirk Gibson, tongue in cheek, how it felt to be playing in his very last football game. (I still didn't believe he was going to choose baseball over football.)

"Keith, this *is* my last football game. And I plan on making it a memorable one."

He sure did. He went out and caught a bunch of balls. Several of the ones I remember seemed impossible: his body was parallel to the ground, his hands just barely grasping the ball in his fingertips as he was pummeled by several headhunting cornerbacks. He hung on to all of them and was named the game's offensive MVP, despite the fact that our North squad lost to the South by 20 points.

I still think he would have made one heck of an NFL wide receiver.

Chapter 7

Hey, Big Guy!

For me, the "big guy" phenomenon started the summer before my sophomore year in college. After years of being a tall and skinny kid, I was finally starting to fill out my six-foot, five-inch frame. I had reached that height more than four years prior, most of it in a growing spurt at the beginning of high school. Now, at age 18, the rest of my body was finally starting to catch up.

My good friend Billy Glenn, who played football at Lehigh University, got us jobs that summer at Joe Namath's football camp in Dudley, Massachusetts. It was such a thrill for us to be there. Besides Joe, the other resident pros included Phil Villipiano of the Oakland Raiders and Winston "Winnie" Hill and John "Doc" Dougherty of the New York Jets. At first I was a bit intimidated by all the famous names and faces, but those feelings were very short-lived. Never have I met a more genuine, down-to-earth bunch of fellas. It was that experience that first put the notion in my head that, yeah, maybe I too could do what they do.

"Broadway" Joe Namath was a huge celebrity by then and already had established himself as one of the greatest quarterbacks ever to play the game. I'll never forget the first time he took a snap from me. He had set up a "seven-on-seven" passing drill—a football practice drill featuring seven receivers versus seven defenders—with some of the other pros and college players after the kids' afternoon workout. Joe announced he wanted to take a snap from center to better help him simulate a game situation. Being the only center in the group, I was nominated. I reluctantly walked out to the middle of the practice field, scared to death I was going to injure those million-dollar hands. I had been switched to the center position during my first spring practice at Penn State just a few months prior and wasn't all that confident in my snapping ability.

Joe yelled out the routes he wanted his receivers to run and announced the play would start on "two."

"Two-fourteen, two-fourteen, set . . . hut, hut," yelled out the All-Pro, Super Bowl hero, future Hall-of-Famer, and current New York Jet.

Next morning's potential sports page headlines flashed before me: "Penn State Sophomore Doofus Lineman Breaks Namath's Fingers: Joe Out for Year."

On the second "hut" I propelled the football up and backward, hoping that they snapped the ball in the pros like they did at Penn State.

Snap! I heard the ball hit his waiting hands.

I turned around to watch Joe shoot a perfect spiral rocket to one of his split ends dashing across the middle.

"Nice snap, Keith," he said with a smile, before barking out the next play to a fresh set of receivers. His hands weren't broken. And he remembered my name! I retrieved another ball, got down in my stance, and fantasized I was playing center for the New York Jets at Shea Stadium, the legendary Namath refusing to enter a game without his trusted center Dorney at the ready.

Joe not only immediately put me at ease that afternoon but turned out to be one of the most pleasant, enjoyable guys I have ever been around. He treated me, as well as everyone else, as an equal, and we all coached, worked out, and partied together throughout the summer. He made it a special time for me and Billy, and I'll always remember that camp as one of the best experiences of my young life.

After putting the campers to bed, it was tradition for the staff to go out on the town for a beer or two. Joe often joined us and handled the inevitable adulation, autograph requests, and often bothersome inquiries like a true gentleman. He always had a smile for everyone and never lost his cool.

He got a real kick out of me one night when I bought him a Johnnie Walker Red. I had read his biography, *I Can't Wait Until Tomorrow . . . 'Cause I Get Better-Looking Every Day*, back in the sixth grade and had remembered that was his drink of choice. His book went on and on about him spending glamorous evenings partying up and down Broadway, armed with a beautiful woman and a Scotch (always Johnnie Walker Red), and it had made quite an impression on me. But whenever he was out with us, he drank beer like everyone else, and I guess I was a bit disappointed. He accepted the drink graciously, although I don't think he really wanted it.

After a few beers, we'd always end up at the local Dunkin' Donuts shop, where Paul Mastroquhoba, the weight coach for the Jets, would start into his routine.

Paul was a pioneer in his trade and added both bulk to my frame and know-how to my brain that summer, but I'll always remember him best behind the counter of that donut shop in Dudley.

He was a diminutive man, especially compared to some of the behemoths seated around the counter, with a clean-shaven crown and muscular build, his face accentuated by a large bushy mustache. He always reminded me of one of those old black-and-white pictures of 19th-century strongmen, with their shaven heads and handlebar mustaches.

We'd all be sitting there—me, Billy, Joe, Phil, Winnie, Doc, and whoever else was in town. Famous celebrities from around the league would constantly drop by, some for a day or two, others for a whole week. It was incredible.

On cue, Paul would emerge from the back, donning an apron and hat, and start into his act. I heard he'd been doing this same routine for years, but you'd never know it from the huge belly laughs it elicited from Joe and the boys.

Now, Paul's skit was sort of funny, but the way everyone carried on you'd think it was the most hilarious thing these guys had ever seen. I mean, guys were literally in the aisles, bent over with laughter. At first, Billy and I looked at each other in wonderment, trying to figure out what we had missed. We came to understand it was more about bonding, tradition, and camaraderie, and after a few days we ended up right there in the aisles with everyone else. The fact that we had drunk a beer or two beforehand probably had something to do with it as well.

"What'll it be for you, sir?" he'd ask in the same convoluted fake accent he used night after night.

"Coffee and a donut, please," his "victim" would respond.

"Better check it first," Paul would reply, picking up a donut and tapping it on the countertop, while simultaneously tapping underneath the counter with the fist of his other hand.

"'At one's a bit stale," he'd say very seriously, as everyone in the shop howled. "Better try another one."

The process was repeated over and over. Locals stopped outside the big picture window, gazing in at the spectacle in amazement, wondering what could possibly be so hilarious. The owner of the shop, who always welcomed the intrusion, would set off baking us fresh donuts and pastries, custom ordered, and we'd often go back in the kitchen to help him.

One particular night, a donut-eating contest was staged. After everyone else had dropped out at around 20 donuts, I kept going, and before long Joe and the rest of the boys, who never needed much of an excuse to have a good time, were once again whooping, hollering, and carrying on like it was the fourth quarter of the Super Bowl. They watched in amazement as I continued to put them away. I finally stopped at 50, my young frame going over the 270-pound mark (the unofficial "big guy" barrier) for what was probably the first time—although a good deal of that weight was undigested dough sitting there uneasily in my gut.

Greg Buttle, an All-American teammate of mine my freshman year at Penn State, was a top draft choice of the Jets that year. I ran into him the following year, after his rookie season. The first thing he told me was that on the first day of their summer camp, Namath came over to him and asked if he knew *me* and was he aware that I held the unofficial Dudley, Massachusetts, donut-eating title. I was blown away that Joe would even remember me, much less the donut incident. But that's just the kind of guy he is.

Ever since Joe's camp, a big guy I was forevermore. "Hey, big guy. You must be either a football player or a professional wrestler," would be a typical inquiry. Wherever I went, people didn't necessarily recognize my face but instantly recognized me as a big guy, who must be that large for some famous reason or another. I loved the attention at first, but as I continued to mature and gain weight and breadth, I started to feel more and more like a freak, and it began to wear on me. Anonymity was no longer possible. Again, being an offensive lineman, I was nowhere even near being a celebrity, and few people recognized my face outside of Detroit, Penn State, or my native Eastern Pennsylvania. But gone were the days when I could slip into a restaurant for a quiet dinner, wander amongst a crowd at the mall, or enjoy a quiet day at the beach.

The inevitable questions would arise, and soon my "cover" would be blown and my privacy lost. Sure, I enjoyed my newfound status for a few years, but it wasn't long before I yearned to be "normal" again and bask in being just another Joe (not Namath), something that most of us take for granted.

I can only imagine what it would be like to be a real celebrity, to have a face that was instantly recognized wherever you went, never being able to go anywhere without being constantly hounded. Being a big guy for a large chunk of my life gave me just a taste of what that must be like. I would imagine it would get to be a real bummer after a while.

Being branded a big guy was part of my motivation for immediately losing a bunch of weight after retiring from the game. I'm happy to say that I now weigh in somewhere around 230, well under big-guy status, and move around freely—unhindered and unnoticed—under the radar of big-guy watchers everywhere.

Traditionally, after Thursday's practice during the NFL football season, which usually was the last day of heavy hitting, there would be an offensive line "meeting." It was held each and every Thursday during the season, and attendance was mandatory for all of the Lions' offensive linemen. These meetings were usually held at one of Detroit's seedier bars, and it was an opportunity for the linemen to have a few cocktails together, bitch about the coaches and management, and generally bond as a unit.

The venue never stayed the same for more than a week or two. Having 10 or 15 drunk patrons in your bar, each of whom weighed over 270 pounds, wasn't necessarily a good thing. Offensive linemen, generally speaking, are very sensitive to the needs of the people who pour their beer.

Depending on our mood, but probably more so on our win-loss record at the time, the meeting site would be purposely very obscure or at other times openly public. Offensive linemen, generally speaking, are also a rather thrifty group, regardless of salary, so cheap beer was desirable. These rules were occasionally broken in fits of reckless spending, mostly after a big win, where a lavish dinner, an expensive nightclub, or even a limousine-chauffeured junket across the river to Jason's, an all-nude bar in Windsor, Ontario, was indulged.

Upon his arrival from the Philadelphia Eagles, offensive lineman Steve "Red Man" Kenny had dubbed these Thursday nights "Attitude Adjustment Night," or simply "AA," the name they had used for it back in Philadelphia. AA it was forevermore.

Let me interject a word of caution here. If you ever happen to be in an NFL city, and you run into one of these AA gatherings, please, for your sake, *do not* try to drink with any of these men.

Offensive linemen are probably the most approachable members of a football team, and we often had fellow patrons interested in talking with us, buying us beer and shots, and generally getting caught up in the whole testosterone thing. What they didn't realize is that offensive linemen drink like fish. And a 300-pound fish can hold his liquor a lot better than a fish half his size. We consistently had these well-wishers barfing on their shoes, their machismo getting in the way of good old common sense.

Another word of caution. If you happen to be introduced to one of these individuals, shake his hand gently.

Everyone who plays professional football, except for kickers, is extremely vulnerable to thumb, finger, and hand injuries. The players whose hands are usually in the worst shape, though, are the offensive linemen. And they get worse as the season progresses. Old hand injuries never have a chance to heal, and new ones are added every week. You can always tell an offensive lineman from his mangled, broken, and swollen fingers.

In the course of doing the job, a lineman is constantly bashing digits against an opponent's hard helmet, shoulder pads, or face mask. It's also common to get a finger caught in the ear hole of a helmet or in a face mask, or tangled up in a jersey while wrestling around with an opponent. This often results in a broken, sprained, or dislocated finger or thumb.

Worse, getting your hand or fingers caught in between two helmets during a violent collision can be particularly painful and damaging. If you've ever accidentally whacked your thumbnail with a hammer, then you know what I'm talking about. Pressure builds up behind the nail, and a small hole must be made in it to release the tremendous force of the hemorrhaging behind it. Our longtime trainer, Kent "Tweety" Falb, would hoard copper paper clips in his desk drawer for just this reason (copper heats up hotter than regular metal).

After heating the clip until it glowed red hot, the tip of it was plunged into the nail, making a small hole. I once had blood shoot out nearly a foot in the air from a particularly gruesome thumbnail. Man, did that ever feel good! It's amazing how much a little thing like a thumbnail can cause so much pain. Not unlike the proverbial lion getting a thorn stuck in his paw.

Near the end of my career, someone invented a machine that took away any guesswork involved with the paper clip method. The machine heats up a needle, then precisely controls the depth of the plunge, preventing it from traveling too far into the flesh beneath the nail, as often happened with the paper clip.

Although this new machine worked well, it wasn't nearly as much fun. I know Tweety was disappointed. He grew up an Iowa farm boy and prided himself on his collection of good old-fashioned horse-sense remedies. The machine was just another concession to modern medical technology.

Please, *don't try the paper clip method at home*, unless you are a trained professional, have passed Paper Clip Heating 101 (available through finer junior colleges across the country), or are one incredibly sick bastard. Inevitably, one of you will be in galactic pain one evening after whacking a finger with a hammer, dropping a brick on a toe, or some other boneheaded maneuver. You'll recall Tweety's neat little trick I've described here and feverishly start rummaging through your stash of paper clips, looking for that magic copper one like some stressed-out addict. Desperate to relieve the pain but too cheap to go to the emergency room, you'll heat up the wrong type of paper clip, push the metal too far into the nail, or make some other rookie civilian mistake. Tweety and I accept no liability for these actions.

So, when shaking an offensive lineman's hand, be sure to squeeze very gently. Personally, I can recall just the opposite happening many times. It was always the same scenario. I would get introduced to a stranger and he'd offer me his hand to shake. Reluctantly, I'd offer my hand in turn, warning the gentleman of my injured hand and to please, *please*, not squeeze very hard. Excited to meet a pro football player and looking at the size of me, he'd immediately dismiss my warning, squeeze the hell out of my hand, and then wonder why the big tough guy was doubled over, holding his hand in pain.

It was at one of these AA meetings that a detailed discussion of the big-guy phenomenon broke out. In the midst of our session, someone asked the question: "How many times in your life have you been called 'big guy'?" No one seated around the table weighed less than 270 pounds, so the response was unanimous that it had been *way* too many times.

Karl Baldischwiler, our left offensive tackle, suggested that "big guy" should be tailored more specifically to the individual. "Big Tex" was almost immediately branded on Doug English, our perennial All-Pro defensive tackle. That was an easy one. English grew up in Texas, was an All-American at the University of Texas, and looked, dressed, and acted like he was from Texas. Plus, he was pretty damn good-looking for a big guy, with a soft southern drawl that made the ladies melt.

Now, Doug was a defensive player and technically shouldn't have been at our meeting; however, offensive linemen as a group are generally a very amiable lot, and we of course welcomed any team members who cared to join us. That is, except kickers. We had to draw the line somewhere.

We especially loved it when our quarterback attended AA. It gave us a chance to bond with the man whom we were paid to protect. Also, the quarterback always thought it was in his best interest to keep us happy and would almost always pick up the tab. Personally, it didn't make any difference to me. I mean, I had a job to do, and I was going to do it to the best of my ability no matter what, and whether or not the guy back there did or didn't buy me a beer the previous Thursday night didn't actually factor into the effort I put forth into my pass protection. Naturally, I always kept this fact to myself. A free beer is a free beer. Plus, quarterbacks made a hell of a lot more money than I did.

Baldischwiler, the man who brought up the big-guy branding in the first place, was next. Again, he was an easy one. He grew up in Oakmogee, Oklahoma, played for the Sooners at the University of Oklahoma, and was never without a "dip" between his cheek and gum. He wore cowboy boots and Stetson hats and looked so much like Hoss

Cartwright from *Bonanza* that it was amazing to everyone in the room that no one had ever called him "Hoss" before. He was always "Big Hoss" after that, or at least until he was traded to the Indianapolis Colts later that year.

I was next. For no particular reason, the newly crowned Big Tex stood up, pointed at me, and blurted out: "Well, that must make Dorney the 'Big Cheese'!" The room erupted with laughter, and my nickname was born. The "Big" was soon dropped, and for the rest of my career I would be known as just "Cheese." Not the most flattering of nicknames, and quite irreverent, but I never minded. Eventually, everyone called me that—players, coaches, and staff members alike. I suspected that some of the younger players didn't even know my real name. Some even referred to my wife, Katherine, as "Mrs. Cheese."

The next week, I had the pleasure of attending an impromptu bash at Al "Bubba" Baker's house.

Baker, the Lions' right defensive end, was the most prolific cog in the Detroit Lions' famed "Silver Rush," the nickname for the four down defensive linemen, of whom the aforementioned Big Tex was a part.

In their day, the Silver Rush could really rush the passer and cause some serious problems for opposing offenses, especially in the noisy Pontiac Silverdome. Bubba and Dave Pureifory would bring it from the ends, and Big Tex and the late John "Woody" Woodcock would bring pressure from the inside. Bubba, Big Tex, and Pureifory still rank in the Lions' top 10 all-time list for sacks in a season, with Bubba holding down the top three slots with 23, 16, and 18 sacks in consecutive seasons (1978–1980). The Silver Rush, although not as famous as the "Orange Crush" or the "Purple People Eaters," was a formidable force for many years in the late seventies and early eighties.

In his heyday, Bubba was unstoppable. He stood six feet, seven inches, at times weighed up to 270 pounds, and had long nimble arms with an iron grip. The Silverdome scoreboard would flash "Kill Bubba Kill" whenever there was a crucial defensive third down. The raucous crowd, all eighty thousand of them, would stand and scream, making it impossible for the opponent's offensive tackles to hear the cadence, thus enhancing Bubba's chance for a sack.

Not that he needed any help. When he was in his prime, Bubba had an incredible array of weapons at his disposal. He would line up four yards outside his opponent's left offensive tackle and angle himself toward the quarterback. With all of his weight forward on his down right hand, he would explode off the line of scrimmage the instant he saw the offensive center move the football.

He could beat you upfield with a speed rush. Many times an offensive tackle wouldn't even be able to lay a hand on Bubba as he breezed by him on his way to the quarterback. He could run over you, fake his deadly outside rush and go inside, or release one of a countless collection of spin moves that he worked so hard on in practice.

I've played against some really incredible defensive ends in my time: Reggie White, Jack Youngblood, Ed "Too Tall" Jones, Howie Long, Mark Gastineau, Claude Humphrey—the list goes on and on. It's my opinion that during his prime, from around 1978 to 1981, Bubba could rush the passer better than *anyone.*

Although his productivity had waned some by this time, it was due more to the fact that he was just plain fed up with the Lions' lack of success, and I think he was more bored than anything else. He started quarreling with the coaches, became disenchanted with his salary, and had been showing up to camp out of shape. But Bubba was indifferent. He loved to have a good time, and the coaching staff could go fuck themselves for all he cared.

Inspired by a James Brown song on the stereo and a few beers, Bubba started dancing and singing, oblivious to my presence on his couch.

I feel good, na nah na nah na nah na. I knew that I would, now, na nah na nah na nah na.

His huge mastiff, cleverly named Bubba as well, was also attending the party and joined Bubba in the dance. He placed the dog's massive paws on his shoulders, and the two Bubbas started to groove.

Like sugar and spice, darlin', na nah na nah na nah na.

Bubba the dog seemed to enjoy the dancing and the extra attention he was getting from his master. By this time, Bubba had put on his sunglasses, and he and the dog swayed back and forth, back and forth as one, Bubba and Bubba moving and jiving to the beat.

By this time, everyone in the room was watching them, and all eyes could not help but follow Bubba the dog's massive balls, swaying back and forth as the two danced.

Fresh from the previous week's big-guy discussion and a beer or two, I blurted out, "Hey, looky there, it's 'Big Sexy'!"

The place erupted with laughter, and Big Sexy, who loved an audience, and Bubba the dog danced on.

So good! Bomp bomp. So right! Bomp. I got you, Bah Bah Bah Bah Bah!

Big Sexy, although a great nickname, didn't really stick. He already had a nickname—Bubba—and Bubba's days as a Lion were also numbered.

It warms my heart to get called Cheese these days, with or without the "Big" adjective, which is limited mostly to reminiscing on the phone with old teammates or the occasional minireunion. It reminds me of my playing days and my teammates, both big and nonbig guys alike.

If I've been extra good, sometimes my wife will humor me and call me the Big Cheese.

Chapter 8

Bark like a Dog

To reach the pinnacle of your profession, to rise up into the elite top one-quarter of 1 percent, to be able to compete with the very best, sacrifices have to be made, pain has to be ignored, and, most importantly, lessons have to be learned. It's a mental, not a physical, thing that sets the great ones apart from the good ones, the elite from the mediocre, the winners from the also-rans.

The above rings true for practically any undertaking—academics, business, parenting, or horseshoes. There are very few who can achieve success without first undergoing sacrifices. In most cases, the level of success is commensurate with the effort one is willing to put forth. Depending on the endeavor, this could translate into long days and nights at your start-up business, enduring hours and hours of tedious repetition as an intern, or late nights studying, holed up deep behind the stacks of books at your university's library.

As an NFL football player, this translated into stomaching hours upon hours of grueling physical training, both during the season and in the off-season. Especially in the off-season, physical conditioning and strength training had to be the paramount focus. Those unwilling to put in this time never reached their full potential, or never made the grade in the first place.

Are there other skills needed to play in the NFL? Naturally, speed, quick feet, flexibility, toughness, and a knowledge of the game are all essential ingredients. However, I have always felt that improving your physical conditioning and gaining strength—no matter what your position (kickers exempted)—would make you a better football player.

In-season conditioning and strength training were necessary as well, especially considering the grueling 20-game NFL schedule. We're talking survival here. You've got to stay healthy and play every week to make it. Countless talented football players, with limited success in the NFL because of injury, can attest to that. In addition, what's the use of making gains in the off-season, only to lose it when you need it most?

I never would have been able to accomplish what I did if not for the help of a group of individuals—mentors, coaches, and workout partners—who helped persuade, cajole, and sometimes force me to do what I needed to do, pushing me to new limits, helping me set aside the pain.

Macungie Mountain, Fall 1973

I set off at a slow jog from my house on Main Street in Macungie, Pennsylvania. It didn't take me long to get out of town. Through my backyard, underneath the walnut tree, across Chestnut Street, through the baseball diamond adjacent to the firehouse, across little-used Cotton Street, and there it was, looming in front of me, challenging, beckoning, calling to me.

Technically, it wasn't really a mountain. According to the U.S. Geological Survey, to qualify as a mountain it would have to stand 2,000 feet above sea level. Macungie Mountain, part of the Alleghenies of Eastern Pennsylvania, stood just over 500 feet. Not even close. But that's what everyone called it. Macungie Hill just didn't sound right.

I couldn't have cared less about those details at the time. I was 15 years old, in the midst of my junior year in high school, and as far as

I was concerned, it was Mount Everest, appearing insurmountable and unconquerable.

I had hiked up it and beyond countless times before, but this was the first time I, or anyone for all I knew, had ever thought of trying to run up it. I was determined to give it my best shot.

A gravel road, well maintained by the Borough of Macungie, snaked its way up the mountain to the town's reservoir, which was the source of drinking water for the residents. My goal was to run to the end of that road.

The reservoir itself was unique. It was a fully enclosed structure, with wood siding and a metal roof, perched on the side of a hill about three-quarters of the way up the mountain, just below the natural springs that fed it. It was small, like the town it served, and blended in wonderfully with its natural surroundings, nestled in a grove of pine trees, surrounded by native oak, maple, and beech.

I had a considerable distance to cover—and pain to endure—before I reached the reservoir. Old Carwood Grove appeared to my right, along with the pond that the other local kids and I kept stocked with trout, bass, and sunfish. Over the years, we'd catch fish in the many surrounding bodies of water—creeks, farm ponds, and lakes—and transplant them to our local fishing hole. Long ago, someone had thrown a goldfish of some sort in there, and it had grown to immense proportions. It would show itself occasionally, adding to its legend, making the fishing that much more exciting. I've never heard of anyone ever catching it.

In the summer, it was our own personal fishing and swimming hole. In the winter, we'd shovel off the snow and play ice hockey, fashioning hockey sticks from fallen branches found in the woods.

On my left, nestled next to the forest, hidden behind a hedgerow, was the original "field of dreams." We had no idea who had built it or how it was maintained, and frankly, we didn't care. At times, the baseball diamond would be wonderfully groomed and pristine, and at other times overgrown and unkempt. I never saw anyone use it but us. It was always there for us over the years, whenever the mood struck us to conjure up a baseball game.

The warm autumn sun disappeared abruptly as I entered the trees, the air cool and crisp, heavy with the wonderful smells of the forest. My lungs started to burn as the modest incline turned steeper. I forded the small creek that skirted across the road and ran on.

The previous Friday night, my football team, the Hornets of Emmaus High School, had hosted the always tough Concrete Kids of Northampton. It was a glorious game, played under the lights and attended by thousands of fans from both sides. I had played both offense and defense for the Hornets, as well as some of the special teams, and I had never been so tired in all my life. I had decided right then and there that I was going to do something about that, thus my early-Sunday-morning run. I was determined to increase my endurance so I could concentrate on playing football, rather than merely surviving.

Sweat was now flowing freely from my pores as I navigated the turns, the grade getting steeper and steeper the closer I got to my goal. The soft gravel and dirt gave way beneath my feet as I ran, further impeding my progress and frustrating my now monumental efforts.

I could see the end through the trees now, about 150 yards ahead. But my leg muscles were burning, my lungs heaving, and the remaining grade seemed impossibly steep. I wasn't sure I was going to make it, but I was determined to try.

I was barely moving, even though my arms and legs were pumping furiously, as I passed an oblong granite marker on my left. On one side was the inscription "Macungie Water Shed." The side visible to me had "1895" carefully engraved on its face.

When I finally reached the end of the gravel road and the top of the reservoir building, my legs were wobbly, and I had never before been so winded. It wasn't pretty, but I had made it.

I caught my breath and hiked farther up the hill. The natural springs, somewhere up the boulder-strewn hillside, provided a steady stream of cold, clean water for the residents of Macungie. It cascaded down, through, around, and in between the intricate crevices, creating tiny but spectacular waterfalls. I carefully hiked between the pools of water that formed where the pitch of the mountain allowed. These pools provided a habitat for salamanders, tadpoles, and water bugs and over the years provided hours of fun-filled critter-hunting for my friends and me.

The sound of water on rocks was everywhere. It got louder as I carefully made my way farther up the hill and over the water-slick rocks. It enveloped me, embracing me in its roar.

Suddenly, there it was, appearing out of nowhere, an oasis in a sea of sharp angles and steep cliffs. A flat, nearly level rock, surrounded on all sides by cascading water, invited me to sit and rest my weary body. I did just that. I reveled in the afterglow of my run. I thought about last Friday's football game and what I could do better next week. I reflected on my young life and wondered what the future might hold.

As I sat there, the only thing I heard was the rushing of water, which literally surrounded me on all sides. Cool mist caressed my face, and I could feel the dampness of the air on my bare arms, legs, and face. I got up and stuck my head under a waterfall and was surprised by the coldness of it. Then I drank. The water, sweet and pure, tasted so good.

That smooth, flat rock, my rock, is a special place. And so is Macungie Mountain—my first training partner.

In subsequent years I would make that same run literally hundreds of times. As I got older, I began timing my runs with a stopwatch, pushing myself to go faster and faster each time. When I was training for my college seasons, I would walk back down to the oblong granite marker and repeat the most difficult, steepest part of the run over and over again.

After every run, I would return to my rock.

And drink in that cold, clean, magical water.

The Basement, Allentown, Pennsylvania, YMCA, Winter 1973
I walked down the steps and was immediately overwhelmed by the smell—a musty, sweaty, human smell—that was unique to the basement of the "Y." Although I'd been down here on and off the past few years, lately I'd been steadfast in my workouts, determined to add muscle to my tall and skinny body. For over a month now, my mom had faithfully dropped me off, then picked me up an hour and a half later, three times a week.

Unlike our high school weight room, which consisted at the time of merely a single universal gym, the Y had a "real" weight room. It was dimly lit. Racks of dumbbells lined the walls, ranging in weight from 5 to 120 pounds. Unlike most gyms of that era, this one was outfitted with Olympic bars and tons and tons of Olympic weights. Squat racks, flat benches, and inclined benches dotted the floor, reflected in the mirrored walls. A set of handmade chin and dip bars, fashioned from steel and bolted to the wall, adorned one corner.

It was spotless. The patrons kept it that way. All the equipment was clean, oiled, and well maintained by the regulars. A lot of the stuff was theirs, not the Y's. And you never saw weights strewn around the floor or out of place. It just wasn't tolerated.

Although I had gotten used to the smell, I was still having trouble adjusting to the people. Men, *real* men, with big muscles and bad attitudes, worked out down here. The mostly blue-collar crowd didn't tolerate any sissy-lah-lah types, kids, or anyone else that wasn't serious about working out. Last week, I looked on in horror as two of these behemoths worked out a disagreement. No "baseball fights" down here. It was the real thing. The donnybrook lasted nearly a half hour. It started in the weight room, spilled over into the adjacent room housing the universal gym, and finally ended badly in the wrestling room, where one of them had finally gotten the upper hand and was bashing the other's head against the concrete block wall. Only then did anyone step in to stop it. Both were bloodied badly. To their credit, the two were back working out tonight, the cuts adorning their faces healing nicely, although they did appear to be keeping their distance from each other.

Between high school and basketball, I could only come down here later in the evening, during a specific time period, and I was getting to know the crowd of regulars that frequented the place. Not personally—not one of them had even so much as spoken a civil word to me—but by observation and reputation.

One of them, I never did catch his name, hated bodybuilders, which he considered anyone who wasn't a power lifter or an Olympic lifter like himself. He was huge, well over 200 pounds, with big thighs and gargantuan arms. He stuttered when he talked and was constantly muttering the phrase "f-f-fucking b-b-bodyb-b-builders" to anyone he thought was acting inappropriately. I steered *way* clear of him.

Mike Boyer, a former local football legend, also was a regular. Although short by Y weight-room standards, he was incredibly strong and powerful. I once saw him do 35 perfect chin-ups. From what I heard, he still played "knucklehead" football regularly, which was 11-on-11 football, *without* helmets or pads.

Then there was Billy Whiteknight. His reputation preceded him. A former member of the local motorcycle gang The Pagans, it was rumored he had killed several men once in a fistfight and wouldn't hesitate to do the same to you if you didn't watch your step. He reminded me of a large grizzly bear, with a bushy red beard, furry forearms and legs, and hair down past his shoulders. He had traded in his Harley for a huge, powerful pickup truck with a steel beam fashioned as the front bumper and had taken up power lifting as a hobby. He stood over 6'0", weighed close to 300 pounds, and appeared to be able to bench-press and squat the world. When he worked out, the bar looked as if it would break in half from all the weight he loaded onto it.

There was a strictly enforced, unwritten conduct code that I was learning the hard way. I had been chastised and embarrassed many a time these last few weeks, unwittingly not putting away a piece of equipment properly, leaving a bar on a bench, or disrupting someone's superset.

"Hey, kid, you working arms tonight?"

At first I thought the tall, bespectacled, muscular man was talking to someone else, but then I realized I was the only kid in the room. I had seen this guy down here often. He never said a whole lot and worked out like a lunatic. I was trying to work my arms that night, copying the exercises the other men were doing, but I was having trouble, not possessing the know-how or expertise to master them properly. I was embarrassed by my long, thin arms and yearned to develop big "guns" like the other guys in the room.

"Ah, yeah, I guess," I replied sheepishly.

"We're doing a superset here, here, and here," he pointed. "You know what a superset is? It's when you do one exercise and then go right to another and then another. We call that one set. We'll do the whole thing three times total. What's your name?"

"Keith."

"Keith, this is my partner, Roger." Roger glared at me. He didn't utter a word, nod his head, or acknowledge me in any way. My first impression was that he wasn't too keen on letting the kid screw up his workout routine.

"Roger here will go first. Watch what he does, and try and copy him. Then you go. I'll go last."

Roger didn't say much, but man, did he work hard. He, too, was tall and muscular but had more of an edge to him, a "don't fuck with me or I'll kill you" type of persona. He had a bushy dark beard and always wore combat jungle boots when he trained.

As I watched Roger finish up his first set and saw the intensity he put into every repetition, I knew right then and there this wasn't going to be easy. These guys were working out at an entirely different level than me.

When it was my turn, the nameless man with the glasses grabbed the bar in his powerful hands and showed me the proper path it should take. He adjusted my grip and told me to scoot up on the bench. I did what I was told and tried not to protest when, on the next set, he not only added more weight to the bar but made me do about four more repetitions than I thought I could.

When I woke up the next day, my arms were so sore and stiff I could barely wash my hair in the shower. But it was a good hurt. I knew I had worked hard and had gotten something done. I showed up the next night at the regular time, more eager than ever.

"Hey, kid, we're doing chest and shoulders if you want to work in."

"Hey, thanks. Yeah, I'll work in."

After an hour, I was covered with sweat. I had never worked out so hard in all my life.

"We're working legs tomorrow, so make sure you get a good night's sleep."

"I'll be here."

"By the way, my name's Mike. Mike Holenda."

We shook hands.

"Nice to meet you, sir."

Mike laughed at my "sir" comment.

He proceeded to take me under his wing the next few months. Roger, at first reluctant to share his workout partner, accepted me as well. He wasn't an ax murderer like I had first suspected, and I realized he hadn't purposefully tried to intimidate me. He was a quiet and introspective man, and that was just his way.

Shortly thereafter, I finally got my driver's license, the basketball season ended, and I was able to make every workout. I got to know the other guys in the gym. Although most of them were a tad demented, it turned out that they were just regular guys.

They joked around with me a lot, teasing the high school kid, but always in a friendly, good-natured way. They taught me the nuances of lifting weights and how to make my body stronger. My body slowly started to transform. I began to gain weight—good weight—and all of a sudden, I wasn't just a tall and skinny kid anymore.

I'll never forget those nights spent down there, our "field trip" to the Cementon Fair, or Mike's willingness to help out a clueless, skinny kid.

The Pontiac Silverdome Players' Parking Lot, Fall 1985

I parked my black Ford Econoline van in the very first spot at the top of the ramp. Like clockwork, just as I was cutting the engine, Chris "Deets" Dieterich's Ford pickup pulled up in the space next to me. There were no other cars. We were the first players to arrive at the Silverdome. There was parking for 70 cars down the ramp by the Silverdome's entrance, but players were forbidden to use those spaces. They were reserved for the coaches, staff, and management only.

We began the 200-yard walk down the ramp to the Lions' facilities slowly, working out our ridiculously stiff and sore bodies. My right thigh was particularly sensitive, the result of a blow of some sort, probably a helmet or a kick from a Minnesota Vikings player. I remembered the play but never did discern where the hit came from—I'd find out when I watched the film in a few hours. This helped offset somewhat my chronically sore left knee as we walked down the steep grade. My back was still screaming, stiff from the previous day's activities and the 15-minute drive from my house in Lake Orion.

Deets' hips, especially the left one, creaked and moaned with each step he took. Both hips were getting worse, but there was nothing he could really do to make them any better, except quit football. He masked the pain—a little bit of it anyway—with cortisone shots and anti-inflammatory pills. The pain began in the left hip midway through his second year with the Lions and had steadily worsened. The right hip began flaring up the following year. There were times yesterday when he could barely pick himself up off the ground. I remember helping him up on several occasions, the pain clearly evident on his stoic, sweat-covered face.

The sky was gray. The massive parking lot was gray. From the mammoth roof of the dome before us, past the endless rows of tenement housing, to the horizon, all appeared to be painted the same dull color.

"I love the smell of worms in the morning. Smells like . . . defeat."

I chuckled at Deets' Robert Duvall impression, his reference to what he knew to be one of my favorite movies, *Apocalypse Now*, and the beating we had taken the previous afternoon at the hands of the Minnesota Vikings.

Side by side, we walked down the blacktopped ramp in the cool, damp Michigan morning. The ramp descended below ground level, surrounded on both sides by steep mounds of dirt. Whenever it rained, as it had last night, thousands of worms came out of their holes to avoid drowning. Many of them ended up on the blacktop, unable to find their way home. Here they perished and filled the air with the pungent scent of the earth.

We both dismissed the worm odor and began to focus our minds on what we had to do. It wasn't going to be easy this morning, but then it never was. That's why we were both already dressed in our workout gear, our street clothes in our bags, which we carried on our shoulders. There was no time to drink coffee in the locker room, lollygag around, or make idle chitchat with the staff. We passed through the air lock door, ignored the entrance to the locker room to our left, and headed straight for the Detroit Lions' weight room.

The weight room was right next to the entrance to the playing field, and both of us, despite our single-mindedness, couldn't resist taking a quick look. The domed arena looked quite different from the way it had yesterday afternoon. The seventy-thousand-plus mass of people was gone, and the Honolulu blue seats glowed eerily in the softened light.

Workers were everywhere, even at this early hour. Some were up in the stands, sweeping up the tons of debris—beer cups, food wrappers, cigarette butts, and other miscellaneous trash. Others were on the field, or what was left of it anyway, busy rolling up the strips of AstroTurf, revealing the gray, hard, unyielding concrete beneath.

The AstroTurf was not one whole piece but actually a series of 10-yard strips that were rolled out width-wise on the concrete for football. The Silverdome was a multiuse facility, and most of its uses called for the turf to be removed. A crew would roll up the turf and move the huge rolls out of the way by forklift to get ready for the next event—concerts, rodeos, basketball games, circuses, truck pulls, you name it—then roll the turf back onto the concrete for football. This nearly constant rolling and unrolling of the turf certainly contributed to its demise. The crew was currently preparing the Silverdome for a rock concert slated for later that week.

Several of the rolls of AstroTurf were sitting near us on the concrete, waiting to be removed. Deets walked over to the one nearest him to scrutinize it more closely, the massive roll dwarfing him in both girth and height. I followed him over.

The turf was actually two separate pieces, the green AstroTurf itself and a white underpadding. Deets examined the pieces, holding them between his thumb and forefinger. The thickness of the two combined wasn't even an inch.

"Hell, why even bother rolling this shit out for the games?" he said, as he further studied the pitiful, crumbling underpadding. "It's not worth the trouble, and the concrete wouldn't cause these damn turf burns." He showed me several oozing, nasty ones that decorated his right arm.

The AstroTurf's thickness and the rock-hard concrete were just part of the problem. The seams, occurring every 10 yards when the AstroTurf was rolled out, didn't fit together nearly as well as they had when it was new. They were supposed to fit together like a glove, with matching tongue-and-groove "lips" running along each side, but they were too deteriorated to fit cleanly. The toes of players had been catching in these lips lately, causing them to trip—or worse.

Players and coaches were outraged a few years earlier when offensive lineman Tom Tenure caught his toe in a seam and blew out the anterior cruciate ligament in his left knee. No one had even touched him. It was like the turf just rose up and grabbed him. In the miniscandal that followed, the Silverdome crew had actually started to sew each seam together for games. This ended up being a monumental task, requiring countless hours of hand stitching, especially considering they had to do it several times a month, sometimes even more. After the furor over the Tenure incident died down, we noticed that they didn't bother sewing the seams anymore, and it was back to business as usual. Except for Tom, of course.

Shaking my head, I turned and walked back off the field. I grabbed the silver handle to the Honolulu blue weight room door, threw it open, and waited until Deets limped through. We both dropped our bags down on the ground by the door and walked across the length of the room to one of the squat racks.

It was a cavernous room, appearing even more so because of the 20-foot ceiling and mirrored walls. Racks, benches, rows of dumbbells, and lots of shiny new equipment were everywhere. A Honolulu blue and silver mural adorned the one wall, depicting what looked like a rodent lifting weights.

The room, in which both of us spent so much time, seemed so dead and lifeless compared to the usual sounds of groaning men, the clanking of metal plates, and the loud, blaring music emanating from the four wall-mounted speakers. But now, the place was all ours, and it was time to get down to business.

We methodically and silently loaded up the 45-pound Olympic bar with the big plates, alternately placing one plate on each end until it was loaded with eight total, four on each side, which made 405 pounds. After securing a lifting belt around his belly good and tight, Deets shouldered the load behind his neck, took a few moments to balance it, and began.

He squatted until his big thighs were parallel to the ground, hesitated a moment, then pushed his way back up. The first ones always hurt the most. He chased the pain out of his head and squatted again. And again. By the time he finished his 30 reps, sweat was dripping off of his nose and onto the floor.

Now it was my turn. Halfway through my set, I was bolstered by the encouraging words of Jim Morrison. Deets had retrieved an old Doors tape from his bag and popped it into the cassette deck.

When the music's over. When the music's over. When the music's over, turn out the lights, turn out the lights, turn out the lights, yeah . . . yeah.

Before I got married, I lived with Deets for a couple of seasons in the same house on the lake where I was currently living with my wife, Katherine. It was there that Deets had turned me on to all of the old Doors tunes: "Waiting for the Sun," "L.A. Woman," "Moonlight Drive," "Light My Fire," "Hello I Love You," "Love Me Two Times."

Deets epitomized the characteristics of the "old-time football player." When it came down to it, I guess I did, too.

We were becoming a rarity in the NFL. It's not that the "kids" coming out of college were any different from us when we were their age. That's not it at all. It's because of the money. These days it was all about the money.

Not that either one of us would go through what we did for free. We wouldn't. And it's not that we weren't well compensated. Both of us were pulling in a decent buck. It's just that things really were so different now than when we had come out of college.

Although I was the 10th player picked in the draft in 1979, my salary that first year was only $35,000. Back then, the owners got to keep most of the money the team generated, and only a relatively small amount was passed on to the players.

By 1985, things were much different. If I had come out of college that year, I would have received a multimillion-dollar signing bonus, the bonus alone setting me up financially for life. Millions of dollars would have been mine before ever strapping on a Honolulu blue and silver helmet.

I wasn't sure that this change was such a good thing. There was no question that I'd rather see the players have the money than the owners, but giving rookie players all that money right away wasn't good for the game. I was convinced that all that cash took away at least some incentive to play hard, to play hurt if necessary, to play football like the game was supposed to be played.

Plus, it pissed us both off that these younger players with less experience and desire were making more money than us, a few of them more than both of our salaries combined. We couldn't help feeling that way. It was just human nature.

I finished my set, my legs wobbly as I set the bar back on the rack. We added more weight, and after a short rest Deets started again. He filled the room with his howls as he finished the set, barely making it back to standing.

By working our legs early in the week, much of their soreness could be worked out. More importantly, it gave our legs time to recover not only from the game but from the heavy leg workout as well, given that Monday was reserved mostly for watching film of the previous day's game and Tuesday was our day off.

Keeping our entire body strong throughout the long NFL season enhanced our performance and protected us from injury. The legs were particularly important, given that knee injuries were so prevalent. Development of the quadriceps and hamstrings, the major muscle groups in the thigh, as well as the gastrocnemius muscle of the calf protected the knee, giving us a better chance for survival.

We realized that this ritual was at least as much psychological as it was physical. It was a way of cleansing our bodies of the previous day's game—shoving it under the mat, so to speak—and getting on to the next opponent. Many times during our early-Monday-morning workouts, which we had faithfully upheld for many years, we would each scream the name of our defensive opponent for the coming week as we finished the last and most difficult reps of our set, knowing full well that our opponent was probably still in his bed.

We continued to alternate sets, adding more weight each time, challenging each other to do more. After finishing the final set, both our shirts and shorts were soaked with sweat, and it also flowed copiously from our faces.

Deets was the starting left offensive guard for the Lions and wore No. 72. Short by NFL standards, he stood 6'2" but weighed in excess of 280 pounds. Since making the team as a fourth-round draft choice in 1980, the sixth-year pro had made quite a name for himself, both on and off the field.

His long, dark-brown hair hung well past his shoulders and this morning was drawn back into a ponytail. His sweat-stained Detroit Lions–issued XXL T-shirt did not adequately cover his XXXL shoulders and arms. He was one powerful man, one of the few people I had ever seen actually bench-press more than 500 pounds.

A walruslike reddish-brown mustache framed his mouth, almost matching the crimson color of his cheeks, which were still flushed from exertion. This intimidating physique was offset by one of the most easygoing attitudes on the squad. Deets was liked by everyone, with the exception of the opponents he played against on Sunday.

One game that stands out in my mind that epitomized Deets' play was when the Dallas Cowboys came to town. The defending Super Bowl Champions thought they were going to have an easy time against us, but they had another think coming. Although I had my hands full with Ed "Too Tall" Jones that day, there was another interesting matchup down the line, where Deets was battling future Hall-of-Famer Randy White. Randy may not have known who Deets was during the game, but you can be damn sure he went and found out afterward.

Randy was one of the strongest players in the NFL, and it was frustrating for him to go up against a guy of comparable strength. The whole game, all I heard after each play was string after string of profanities uttered by Randy toward "No. 72," who more than held his own against him. Deets would come back to the huddle, a big grin on his face, as Randy directed yet another diatribe of cusswords at him. I don't think Deets ever said one word back to him the whole afternoon. He just kept his mouth shut, lined up, and stuck Randy right in the mouth, then came back to the huddle with that big shit-eating grin on his face.

Deets relaxed, knowing the hardest part of the routine was completed, and got another Doors tape from his bag. After putting it into the tape deck, he cranked the volume back up. He sat back down in front of the squat rack on the end of the bench, watching the sweat drip off his nose onto the floor in the full-length mirror, resting for a moment before continuing.

We both sat silently, listening closely to Morrison's rave.

Before I sink ... into the ... big sleep. I want to hear, I want to hear ... the scream ... of the butterfly.

"What the fuck is *that* supposed to mean?" I asked Deets. We both started to laugh.

The drama of yesterday's game, the intense pressure we were under, the mental strain of having to play week after week with a multitude of injuries, the emotional roller coaster we rode each and every week during the football season—it all flowed out, spilling onto the weight room floor.

Our chortles turned to chuckles and then into huge belly laughs. I ended up on the floor. My stomach hurt from laughing so hard.

We sat there, soaking wet from our sweat, panting as we recovered from our spastic laughing attack. We tried to focus back on the task at hand as Jim Morrison finished his impassioned plea. We still had another half hour of legs to finish.

Un ... til the end ... until the end ... until the ... end!

Camp Pendleton Marine Base, San Clemente, California, Summer 1987

It was still dark, a good hour until dawn, but Terry Teale had insisted upon this ungodly hour. He raced his truck up to the guard station, a slightly demented look on his face, a thin smile pursing his lips.

"I want to be on the beach when it's just light enough to see out over the waves. That's when I want to paddle out," he said, as he scrambled to get his Newport Beach firefighter I.D. out of his wallet.

"Permission to use your surf beach, sir," Terry said enthusiastically to the marine standing at attention by the guard tower. They would almost always let Terry in the gate, allowing him motor access to one of the better surf breaks on the Southern California coast—Churches—which was just south of the more popular succession of breaks called Trestles.

The guard gave Terry the once-over. Terry looked like a marine, with close-cropped hair, a ripped body, and an intensity in his eyes with which the guard could probably relate. He glanced in at me, sitting blurry-eyed in the passenger seat, long hair disheveled, a three-day growth of beard on my face. I sat up, trying to not look like a terrorist. Even though I wished I were back in bed, I really hoped he would let us in. It would save us a good 20-minute jog over the sand with our boards to get to Churches, which Terry would insist upon if we were denied access.

The marine instructed me to put on my seat belt, stepped back, and beckoned us on through with a stiff, military-type wave.

"Yes!" Terry exclaimed, as he slowly pulled away from the guard tower. Once we rounded the first bend and were out of sight, he gunned the engine, unable to contain his excitement. I, too, was starting to get stoked. A south swell was supposed to have hit the coast by now, and Terry's overflowing enthusiasm was contagious.

We heard it before we saw it. The unmistakable roar of the ocean greeted us as we wound our way down to the beach. Terry parked in the front row—there was no one else in the parking lot—and we both hopped up on the big piece of timber marking the beginning of the sand. The wind, blowing a good 10 knots, was at our backs.

"This is the kind of day we've been training for," Terry told me with a serious, almost solemn, look on his face. "We're both in good paddling shape. The conditions couldn't be better. We're at one of the best breaks on the California coast. It's going to be epic."

The last couple of times we had gone out together, the waves had been lousy; however, to Terry, that was just an opportunity to get in better paddling shape and get a killer shoulder and cardiovascular workout as well. He had me paddling up and down the coastline until I thought my shoulders and lungs would burst out of my wetsuit. Then he made me paddle some more.

I had met Terry years before at the local gym in Dana Point. He was drawn to me—the intensity of my training getting his attention. He finally had found someone who wanted to work at least as hard as he did in the weight room. We became good friends.

Now, I had a purpose, a reason for pushing my body to the limit. I was striving to get stronger and improve my performance on the football field. If I wasn't playing football, I doubt very seriously I would have subjected myself to the sadistic, almost cruel, workouts we put ourselves through. Terry, on the other hand, was just a sick bastard, plain and simple. Sure, he needed to stay in shape for his job as a firefighter, but that was only part of it. Whatever his motivation, I have met very few individuals who loved to train as hard as Terry Teale.

We proceeded to put on our wetsuits. Even though it was July, the water was still quite chilly. And the sun wasn't due up for another hour or so; it wasn't yet 4:30 in the morning.

As I finished waxing down my board, I looked out over the break and could just barely see the outlines of the huge, clean monster waves rolling in one by one. We walked down to the water's edge and paddled out together into the darkness.

We paddled for what seemed like forever, the wash of the white water pulling us this way and that way, the large breaking waves sneaking up on us through the darkness. My shoulders started to scream from the constant paddling as I "duck-dived" under yet another one.

I was alone now. Terry, who had taught me to surf years ago, was a much better paddler—and surfer—than me. He was out there in front of me somewhere in the darkness, and I was determined to find him, make it outside, and start to have some fun.

Terry had been very patient with me. I did not possess what you would call the typical surfer body, but I was comfortable in the water, had good balance, and possessed a burning desire to learn. He helped me hone my surfing skills over the years and finally had gotten me to this point—a proficient surfer who was able to accompany him to surf any break along the coast. We surfed together a couple of times a week. And, along with Andy Hammel, Mike Whelan, and a few other buds, we would take at least a couple of trips a year deep into Baja, Mexico, where we would camp along the desolate Pacific coast, dine on fresh fish and lobster, and surf our brains out.

I punched through the face of a clean, beautiful, overhead green wall that I should have turned and taken off on, but I was just now starting to be able to see the waves clearly enough in the growing light, rolling out of the darkness, in time to adjust my position. I continued to paddle farther outside for a few more moments then sat up on my board, exhausted, grateful to give my burning shoulders a rest.

"Outside! Outside!" I heard Terry screaming. I snapped my head around and immediately knew it was too late—I was going to get caught inside—again. I could just barely make out Terry, a good 50 yards farther out, demonically paddling toward the horizon, his short frantic strokes taking him up the face of the first wave, then just barely busting through the top of it, swooping down the backside of it before resuming his frantic paddling.

I headed toward the bubbling, swirling mass of white water that was approaching, speeding toward me like some runaway locomotive, its ferocity superseding that of any 320-pound lineman I had ever faced.

With both hands, I reached forward to near the tip of the board and pushed down hard, forcing the front part of it down into the water. I followed it under.

Turn your affections away from Mother Ocean, and she'll make you pay, I thought, as the first rush of water hit the back of my board, which was now nearly perpendicular to the ocean's surface, the three fins, or "skags," just barely sticking out of the water. The force of the powerful wave hitting the bottom portion of my board initially propelled me down and forward, until the buoyancy of the board and my wetsuit stopped my momentum abruptly. The rush of water, less powerful than at the surface but still incredibly strong, now turned me upward, as I breached the surface, popping out of it like one of the many bottle-nosed dolphins that graced these waters.

Although I had avoided the most powerful part of the wave, the remaining white water carried me swiftly backward, eradicating my earlier paddling efforts in one fell swoop. I resumed paddling immediately, which at first slowed my backward momentum, but then propelled me back out to sea as the grip of the wave released me on its way to shore. I stroked hard until I reached the next wall of white water, duck-diving once again, popping up, and again paddling toward the horizon.

I could see Terry on a wave, and I abandoned any further effort in favor of watching him. I sat up on my board to better take in the spectacle. Terry had punched through the first two waves of the set, positioning himself perfectly for what had to be the premier wave of the morning. It dwarfed him as he rocketed down its face and made a smooth, elegant, effortless bottom turn before streaming back up its massive face and violently smashing the lip. He hit the lip twice more, hard, each time causing a prodigious spray, which the stiff offshore breeze transformed into a hundred tiny glistening diamonds. He settled back down, stalled the board slightly by imperceptibly shifting his weight backward, purposely allowing the wall of white water to seemingly swallow him whole, then emerged from it, completely in control.

I watched my friend in awe, his mastery of such a powerful force a beautiful thing to behold.

I whooped at him as he passed, and Terry whooped in return. He'd appear then disappear again and again at the top of the wave before he finally flew back over the top of it, his body and board silhouetted momentarily against the backdrop of the coastal mountains and the emerging dawn, before crashing down into the water in a heap.

He broke the surface, pulled on his leash to retrieve his board, and paddled out to me, a big grin affixed to his face.

We caught more than our share of waves that morning in our two-hour-plus session, the first half of it completely void of other surfers. The early bird not only gets the worm but the tasty waves as well. But we weren't done yet. We were on Terry Teale time, and the day had just begun.

"Teale, I've got to hand it to you. I was not real happy when you roused me out of bed this morning, but that was just about the most fun I've ever had," I said, as we stripped off our wetsuits, both of us totally stoked from our early-morning fun.

"Me too. And what a great cardiovascular workout. And your shoulders look huge. But we still have lots of work to do today. This is just the beginning."

I couldn't help but laugh as I looked at Terry, standing there in the parking lot, beaming, always thinking about his next workout. His long, lean muscles rippled in the early-morning sun. He was shivering, despite the fact that it had warmed up quite a bit, because there wasn't an ounce of insulating fat to be found on his body. His abdomen's six-pack appeared to be painted on his stomach—it was that well defined—and it moved, rippling through his skin like it had a life of its own, as he removed his wetsuit.

We drove to the gym and immediately got to work. For most, the gym was half workout and half social hour, but not for me and Terry.

We were all business and silently went through our well-orchestrated and rehearsed 80-minute back and arm routine. We were both soaked to the bone after finishing our last set.

"What do you say to breakfast at the Harbor House?" I suggested. I was not only exhausted, but famished as well, and felt I could eat most of Dana Point. We gathered a few more takers and walked down the street, choosing a big round table in the back.

The portions were huge, and I devoured my four-egg Mexican omelette, toast, and side of bacon gluttonously. No big shocker there. I weighed in excess of 280 pounds and had just burned more calories than most people did in two days, and it wasn't even 10:00 in the morning. Everyone at the table, however, watched Terry in amazement as he not only finished his own meal but several other leftover ones as well. We had all seen it before, but it was still a source of amazement. How could a guy who weighed 160 pounds, had 3 percent body fat, and was approaching 40 years old, eat like he did and still have a body like a Greek god? The man must have had the metabolism of a hummingbird.

After breakfast, Terry dropped me off at my house and reminded me that our regimen for the day still wasn't complete. I argued with him briefly, but soon gave up. I knew it was no use.

"Look, Keith. You're only two weeks away from summer camp. Now is not the time to be taking days off. I'll see you at Thunder Road at 4:00 P.M. sharp."

"I'll be there," I answered reluctantly, as I retrieved my board and wetsuit from the back of his pickup. I carefully washed out my wetsuit with fresh water and hung it from a hook on the front porch, then went back to bed and slept for two hours, got up, ate, and watched a movie, lying on the couch until it was time to meet Terry again.

Terry, on the other hand, had other plans. His schedule as a firefighter for the city of Newport Beach allowed him time to supplement his working man's wages. He had recently purchased a stump-grinding machine and was off to toil in the hot California sun for the next five hours, fulfilling two appointments he had made the previous week.

Thunder Road, a hill covered with native grass near Terry's condominium in Laguna Niguel, had served us well that summer. By this time in my career, my left knee's cartilage had degenerated badly, and the soft dirt path, combined with a 40-degree incline, allowed me to build up my endurance and cardiovascular fitness with minimal pounding on the knee.

In retrospect, if I had it to do all over again, I could have made some better choices and maybe played a few more years in the league.

My love for the game of basketball certainly hadn't helped my longevity. In the off-season, many years I would play in two separate adult basketball leagues, sometimes playing four games a week. In addition, I would play for hours down on the courts at the beach. All that running and jumping, especially carrying all that weight, certainly contributed to the degeneration of my knees and ankles.

I also enjoyed going on long runs, which was great for my cardiovascular fitness, but my joints could have done without all that additional pounding as well.

However, the overriding factor in my cartilage's demise was the hard concrete floor of the Pontiac Silverdome, and I know many of my former teammates, management, and staff would concur. It took us all a while to figure out that playing, as well as practicing, on that rock-hard surface almost every day—like we did for most of my career—might not be the best thing. At that point, going into my ninth season, the only time we set foot on it was to play our home games. All practices by then were conducted exclusively on grass, which was too little too late for me and some of my teammates. Don't get me wrong. I don't possess any ill will or harbor any animosity toward anyone about my career-ending injury. It was *my* choice, and mine alone, to do the things I did. It just took us all a little while to figure out the obvious with the turf, and hindsight, of course, is 20/20.

It was once again time to tackle Thunder Road, named after the song of the same name by my favorite musical artist, Bruce Springsteen. My dog, named (ironically) Boss, accompanied us for this particular workout, which ended up being our very last. Again and again, Terry pushed me to go up the hill. Boss pissed both of us off, bounding up and down the hill effortlessly, mocking our lowly human efforts. My legs were wobbly and my lungs burned as we walked down the hill for the last time. I thanked him for pushing me so hard that summer. I was as ready as I'd ever been for a football season.

"No, thank *you*," responded Terry.

Later that year, Thunder Road was destroyed, plowed over in favor of more condominiums, forever lost. It was a sign of the times in Southern California: high-density housing replacing meadow, glen, and hillside. But I wouldn't need it anymore anyway. My left knee was too degenerated, too sore, to endure much more NFL football, especially on that damn Silverdome rug.

I've lost touch with Terry since moving with my family to Northern California. I'm sure he's found another workout partner, another surfing buddy, by now. I miss him. There are very few people who can persuade me to get up at 4:00 in the morning to go jump into the freezing-cold ocean.

Even though I don't paddle out these days as much as I used to, I'm still a sucker for a good surfing flick. I dragged my boy Clayton with me to see the premiere showing of *Blue Crush*, a movie I knew contained some great surfing footage. It was filmed on location on the North Shore of the island of Oahu in Hawaii and was about a group of blue-collar surfing women, one of them a budding professional. One particular scene made me think of Terry.

One of the girls was helping to train her friend for an upcoming contest. She made her friend run on the sand on the ocean floor in about 12 feet of water while holding a big rock to counteract her buoyancy. She and another girl floated behind, holding onto their friend's shoulders. The friend would run until her lungs were about to burst, surface to get some air, then repeat the process over and over. It looked to be an intense, sick workout.

I laughed out loud in the theater, thankful that the movie was released after my retirement from the NFL. That's just the kind of thing Terry would have made me do.

Chapter 9

Greatest Hits

"Pig."

Gene Legath, my line coach, spoke calmly and gently, but I knew the manner in which he said it belied how he really felt. His deep-set brown eyes, furrowed brow, and stonelike face read like a book. He didn't have to tell me that this next play was going to determine the outcome of the game. I fed off his unspoken emotions as I looked out onto the field, focusing my attention on my defensive teammates huddled nearly 50 yards away in our opponent's end zone.

As I started to run toward them, fresh adrenaline coursed through my body, transforming the roaring crowd, the heavy drizzle, and the muddy, chewed-up field into some surreal, slow-motion scene from a movie. That scene, however, would never be able to capture the feeling in my gut. Dogged determination, single-mindedness, and fear—a fear as sharp as a razor and very, very real—caused my stomach to turn over and over. I hoped I'd reach my teammates before I retched right there in front of everyone.

I ran and ran, trying to focus only on my mission, which was to stop our opponent from gaining about one inch. That was the distance they needed on this next play to get a first down, which would surely lead to a score and put them in the lead, considering they were on our 3-yard line.

At that moment, nothing else mattered except finding a way to stop them short of that first-down marker. Nothing. I focused my attention back on my teammates and their huddle, their forms becoming clearer as I sliced through the fog and rain.

At first, it looked as if all 10 of them were breathing as one. Every breath they exhaled back into the atmosphere hung above them momentarily, adding to the other breaths already expired, creating a small fog bank there in the end zone.

Their football pants, usually brilliant gold in color, were stained brown by the mud. Splashes of blood pockmarked the pants with a muted red. Four quarters of tough, hard-nosed football takes its toll.

The green jerseys were darker than normal, permeated with perspiration, rain, and the omnipresent mud from the quagmire that by this time barely resembled a gridiron. The only green grass visible was at the far ends of the field, outside the hash marks—the least trampled areas. Every other square foot of the field was brown on brown, and it looked more like a well-used cattle pen than a football field.

My endless run to the huddle, although in reality only a few seconds long, continued. I could start to make out individuals now, not just the group, and my focus sharpened on my teammate Sammy Landis. His breathing was fast and labored, and I watched his expelled air vaporizing as he exhaled mightily again and again. Mud caked his arms, their size belying his round, youthful, cherubic face, which was partially obscured by his double-barred face mask. Our eyes met briefly as I joined the huddle, and I watched splatters of mud melt down his face as the drizzle turned more fierce and the wind whipped into the stadium from behind us.

"Pig! Pig!" I yelled excitedly, as I took my place in the huddle.

Jerry Wenner, our defensive signal caller and leader, stood before us. The black that had been applied below each of his eyes before the game had blurred together with the mud on his face and now mixed with blood flowing from a fresh cut on the bridge of his nose. He appeared exhausted, but one look into his eyes and I knew he was more than up for the challenge of the upcoming play.

"This is it. This drive stops here!" he hissed through his teeth. "Everyone knows what to do. Pig, hard pinch. Ready, break!"

We clapped our hands in unison as we exited the huddle. I immediately got down on my hands and knees and awaited the offensive tackle I had faced all afternoon. He was big and strong and had gotten the best of me most of the day. I was sure they were going to run the ball right at me, just as they had been doing practically the whole game. But this was a new play, and I was determined to do my best to stop that ball carrier.

I lined up on his "outside eye" as he came to the line of scrimmage and immediately got off my knees and into my four-point stance, anticipating a possible quick count. All my weight rested on my fingertips, which sunk downward, disappearing into the slop. I was trying to sell to that tackle that I wanted to go straight ahead, right at him, when in fact I was going to try and shoot his inside gap. My left foot unconsciously raked at the mud, trying to establish some type of foothold.

As their quarterback barked out the signals, I imperceptibly—at least I hoped so, anyway—adjusted my alignment on him from an outside eye to head up, coiling like a giant steel spring whose hair trigger would be released at the slightest movement of the ball to my right, which I kept in my peripheral vision.

That feeling of slow motion overtook me again, and it seemed like the quarterback's cadence went on forever, his voice slowing like it was a recording being played back at one-quarter speed.

When the ball finally was snapped, it almost didn't seem fair. It was like I had an inequitable advantage over my opponents, seeing the scene unfold frame by frame and in crystal-clear clarity. At the initial, almost imperceptible flicker of the center's hand, I pushed hard off my left foot. As the ball moved on its upward arc toward the quarterback's waiting hands, I was already on my way to the gap between their offensive tackle and guard. My jump on the ball was almost as fast as the offensive lineman's in front of me was, and unlike me, he knew the snap count. I burst through the line barely touched by their tackle, who flopped face down in the mud in a vain attempt to block me.

I stumbled forward out of control, all my energy unharnessed after bypassing what I figured would be an inevitable collision with the tackle in front of me. I was still low to the ground—below the butt of the quarterback—who was now right in front of me, his back turned as he handed the ball to his fullback.

That was the last I remember of the play. I have absolutely no recall of much of anything after that moment. I had no idea that I had crashed into both their fullback and quarterback, hitting them around their thighs, upending them as they flew up and over me in a violent collision that ended their play before it even had a chance to begin.

My next recollection was standing on the sideline in front of the visitors' bleachers, which were packed to the brim with our cheering fans.

Our cheerleaders were outfitted in bright gold sweaters, emblazoned in the middle with a big green E juxtaposed over a megaphone, which was outlined in gold trim. Green skirts with gold pleats, white sneakers, and green and gold pom-poms completed their uniform. They were repeating the same cheer over and over again.

"Yeah, Dorney, yeah rah, Dorney!"

The cheer increased in intensity, and I could hear the crowd join in, tentatively at first, then shouting at the top of their lungs as one.

"Yeah, Dorney, yeah rah, Dorney!"

I focused in on one cheerleader in particular. She wasn't her usual smiling self, and I noticed real concern in her eyes. It was then that I first wondered why they were all calling out my name.

"Yeah, Dorney, yeah rah, Dorney!"

I noticed I was swaying back and forth but didn't fall over, being buoyed by invisible forces on each side of me. It was then I saw the ambulance. There is always an ambulance at a football game, but it's

Me and the crew at San Onofre beach in northern San Diego County. From left to right: Terry Teale, Mike Whelan, Andy Hammel, and myself.

Two extremes for my old Ford Econoline van: after an ice storm in Michigan and, three weeks later, halfway down the Baja Peninsula. That's Terry Teale in the cap.

Although football is a physical and at times violent game, you spend a good portion of it on the sidelines—observing, thinking, and strategizing. *Photo this page courtesy of George Gellatly. Photo next page courtesy of the* Detroit News.

My wife, Katherine, and I in Baltimore at the Ed Block Courage Awards in 1986. It was a unique opportunity to party with players like myself from around the league and to meet legendary "old timers" like Johnny Unitas, Art Donovan, and Gene Upshaw.

Chris "Deets" Dieterich and I at a social function. Deets, my former roommate and a great friend, is one of the few people I ever saw bench press over 500 pounds.

usually discreetly tucked away, out of view. This one was right in front of me, at the 50-yard line, on the cinder track that circled the football field. My first conscious feeling since after the hit was one of panic and a need to get back in the game. What was I doing over here on the track while the game was still going on? But the two still-unseen stabilizers, each firmly holding onto my upper arms, prevented me from returning to our bench.

As my senses flickered back to near normal, embarrassment overtook the panic. There was no way I was going to get in that ambulance. I was fine now and didn't want to make a big deal out of whatever had just happened. I had seen my older teammates play hurt, ignore injuries that certainly would have sidelined me, and I wanted to be more like them. I could already hear their jeering, their good-natured taunts, which would certainly be warranted if I needed to get carted away in an ambulance for one little hit to the head. I made another move to return to our bench.

It was then that I saw my dad. He had come down out of the stands, leaving my poor mother sitting up there all alone, in a position of helplessness that would become all too familiar for her in the coming years.

"Hey, Dad. I guess I banged my head a little bit, huh? You'd better get back up in the stands now. I'll see you after the game." I tried vainly to once again return to the bench, but the attending doctor shook his head, smiling as he opened the two big back doors of the ambulance. It was then that I finally noticed Legath, the coach who had sent me into the game just moments before, holding onto my right arm, a look of real concern on his young, handsome face. I watched a drop of rain drip off the tip of his nose, all the while vainly pleading my case as they loaded me, along with my dad, into the back of the ambulance, shutting the double doors with a resounding bang.

I remember sitting down on the crisp, white, clean sheets of the gurney, fretting over how I had just completely soiled them with my drenched, mud-caked uniform.

The ambulance pulled away down the track, its tires making loud crunching noises as it slowly moved through the cinders. The crowd, which was now chanting as one, could still be heard through the walls of the ambulance.

"Yeah, Dorney, yeah rah, Dorney!"

This scene could have been from an NFL game, or maybe a big-time college contest between two rivals, but it wasn't. I was 14 years old, weighed around 160 pounds, and was a sophomore at Emmaus High School in Eastern Pennsylvania.

I played in literally hundreds of football games after that one, but I remember it as well as all the others. Football is like that.

The feelings I had that dreary Saturday afternoon weren't much different than the ones I had when I was playing for the national championship with Penn State six years later, or as a 30-year-old with the Detroit Lions. That's what I tell guys who never played past high school and want to know what it's like to play football at the next level. I tell them that the guys are a bit bigger and a little faster, but other than that, they already *know*.

My senses returned to normal during the ride to the hospital with my dad. Although I had been unconscious for about 30 seconds, didn't remember a thing until I was standing there in front of the ambulance, and had just suffered my first major concussion, I was no worse for the wear, other than having a headache for the next couple of days. My main concern was over the embarrassment I felt, having been carted off the field like that in front of all my teammates and peers. Football games were a big deal then and still are a big deal in that part of the country. *Everyone* was there. I dreaded the next Monday at school, when I would have to face them and be forced to watch the film of the game.

It started immediately that next Monday morning. At my bus stop outside my home in Macungie, Pennsylvania, people who never even acknowledged me before were congratulating me and patting me on the back. No one teased me as I had feared. It continued at school. My manhood, or lack thereof, was never questioned.

Over the weekend, I had been magically transformed from a gangly, socially inept, zit-faced teenager into a popular, well-liked student athlete with near rock-star status—at least for a day or two anyway. I couldn't believe it!

It got even better in the film room. I was much more at ease after being warmly greeted by my older teammates but still dreaded witnessing what I still perceived as my embarrassing moment on film.

The room was completely silent except for the whirring of the 16-millimeter film going through the projector as I sat there alone in the dark, dreading the moment as the play got closer and closer. The first time it ran, it inspired "Ooos" and "Ahhs" from my teammates and coaches. Our head coach Fritz Halfacre, who was running the projector, ran the film back, over and over, without saying a word. I couldn't believe that was me up there on the screen. I had really *leveled* those guys. It didn't hurt that I had done it on fourth down, stopped them well short of the first down, and deprived them of what certainly would have been a touchdown. Plus, we ended up going on to win the game.

After running it back in silence about 10 times, Halfacre finally spoke.

"Men, *this* is how you take an inside gap on a goal-line defense." He ran it back a few more times, as invisible hands reached out and patted me on my back and shoulders. It was one of the few times he had commented on my play all year, and those few words he spoke on my behalf couldn't have been any sweeter.

That incident changed me somehow. It wasn't just my temporarily elevated social status. It was much more than that. It was the hit itself. It felt good. *Real* good. I couldn't wait until the next game so I could try to get another one.

From that moment on, whenever I stepped onto a football field, whether in a game or during practice, I did so with more confidence, more self-assurance. My teammates started treating me with more respect. I quit trying to act like a football player and actually became one, joining a fraternity I didn't even know existed.

I got some more big hits during my high school football career, but none of them equaled that monumental and life-changing one that rainy, cold afternoon at Wilson Borough High School. I came to realize that hits like that don't just occur because you want them to—many variables have to come together to make them happen. Plus, like a lot of things, luck has a lot to do with it.

I got lucky again my freshman year at Penn State. It was then that I first discovered that hatred, a very strong and powerful emotion, could be used to my advantage. Some of that hatred was real, some of it was concocted, but it definitely played into the mix. It all started on a hot and humid summer day in Hershey, Pennsylvania.

I was fortunate enough to be picked to play in a post–high school all-star football contest called the Big 33 Game. The game has a long, rich tradition, and I am very proud to have had an opportunity to play in it. As I mentioned before, Pennsylvania is crazy about football, and the same can be said about Ohio. I'm not saying that there aren't other states that have similar football traditions. Texas, Florida, and California, among others, all churn out incredible athletes who end up filling the rosters of NFL teams on a regular basis. But the Big 33 Game, which pits 33 of the best high school senior football players from Pennsylvania against the 33 best from Ohio, stands alone. There has never been a Super Bowl played that didn't have a Big 33 alumnus on its roster. The game, in one form or another, has been played since 1957. The roster for the Pennsylvania side, as well as our opponents from Ohio that year, was no exception, and years later would read like a who's who of star NFL players.

I must admit, though, I was more than a little intimidated when I first reported to the week-long training camp held in historic Gettysburg, Pennsylvania. I was just 17 years old, and my hometown of Macungie wasn't exactly a large urban area or known as a mecca for football talent. There were players from all over the state, many of them from huge football programs in Philadelphia and Pittsburgh, and I wondered if I was going to be able to measure up.

However, I found out at camp that the coaches at old Emmaus High had prepared me well. Football was football, no matter how big your high school or hometown. Even though I was a little scared, I looked forward to the game, which would be played in Hershey that Saturday night.

My teammates and I were only together for a short time, but we had bonded as a team during our week of two-a-day practices and took great pride in the fact that we would be representing our state in another historic Big 33 Game. That certainly had something to do, I imagine, with my reaction to what happened next.

The night before the game we attended, along with our rivals from Ohio, a dinner given in our honor at a restaurant in Hershey. Afterward, we were relaxing out on the deck, enjoying the warm summer night, when the Ohio squad marched out in unison to join us.

One of their members, Tom Cousineau, had taken off his shirt and strutted before us bare-chested. It wasn't like he discreetly disrobed to catch a few rays. It was an overt and obvious attempt at intimidation.

My first reaction was probably the one that he was looking for, but it was short-lived. Although about my age, his upper body looked like it had been chiseled from granite. I had seen muscular development like that on men before, but this was a boy just out of high school. Even though I was 6'5" and 250 pounds, fear overtook me at the thought of having to go up against him that next evening.

He continued to parade around the deck topless, like some out-of-place peacock, in front of me and the rest of the Pennsylvania players. I conversed in hushed tones about this display with some of my new teammates, who also would be playing against him, and it wasn't long before any fear I might have harbored melted away.

My fear was replaced by outrage. Who did he think he was anyway? One of my more outspoken teammates, a big lineman from Pittsburgh, gathered together me and some of the other boys out there on the deck. He summed up our collective thoughts with a single statement.

"This prima donna asshole is going down!"

I was ready to play some football.

I played both offensive and defensive tackle the next day in the game. When on offense, even though I had my hands full doing my job, I was constantly on the lookout for Cousineau, who played middle linebacker most of the game. I know a lot of my teammates were doing the same, all because of that incident at the restaurant. I never did get the clean shot on him I had hoped for but filed the incident away, like an elephant, for use at a later time.

My next chance came a lot sooner than I had originally anticipated. Cousineau went on to play football at Ohio State. Lo and behold, the Ohio State Buckeyes were scheduled to play Penn State just a few months later.

I was a backup offensive tackle that year as a freshman but played on the special teams, including the kickoff return team. As we watched film on Ohio State the week before the game, I noticed not only that Cousineau was on their kickoff team but that his pursuit lane would be bringing him very close to my vicinity.

I studied the film extra hard that week, conjuring up the incident at the restaurant as extra incentive, and tried to visualize where he would be in relation to me, hoping fate would bring us together. One thing I knew for sure: I wasn't going to go after him unless my assignment dictated it. First and foremost, I was going to do my job. There was no way I was going to put my selfish needs in front of my responsibility to the team—and of course catch bloody hell from head coach Joe Paterno—just to exact petty revenge.

It was a beautiful cold, crisp autumn day that Saturday afternoon at Beaver Stadium, Penn State's home field—perfect for football. As usual, another huge, capacity crowd of seventy thousand-plus fans was on hand, as well as hundreds of thousands more watching on television, to witness what was easily the biggest game of the year for both teams. (Beaver Stadium has been expanded over the years and now holds well over 110,000 fans, and still sells out every game.)

As usual, I was nervous before the game and used every stimulus available to me—my teammates, coach Paterno, the crowd, and yes, the Cousineau incident from months before—as incentive to play to the best of my ability.

After an early score by Ohio State, we were set to receive the kickoff. I was still very nervous—this was my first play of the game—and I pawed anxiously at the natural grass with my spiked football shoes.

As part of the "wedge," it was the responsibility of three of my teammates and me to run back to just in front of the return man receiving the ball and then sprint straight ahead, knocking down anyone in our path. Hopefully, our efforts would create a running lane for our teammate with the ball.

The kick was long and high, and I sprinted back into position. I could feel my fellow wedge members on each side of me as I heard the "go" call from our return man.

Bodies were flying this way and that way on all sides of me as I sprinted straight up the field low and hard, anticipating my chance to throw a block. After what seemed like an endless wait, an Ohio State Buckeye finally appeared in front of me. I didn't know it was Cousineau until the following Monday when I saw the film.

Both of us were running at full speed, aimed directly at each other. I dipped my head slightly just before impact then exploded upward, at the same time maintaining my nearly out-of-control forward momentum.

The collision was tremendous. It was a real "snot-knocker." I caught him right under the chin, and the back of his head was the first thing to hit the manicured grass.

I ended up five yards up the field on my hands and knees, smiling, and tried to track our return man's progress up the field as I stumbled to my feet. But all I could see were stars.

"Seeing stars" is more than just an expression. After an impact to the head such as that one, sometimes all you see, even though your eyes are wide open, is white, punctuated by bright tiny dots, or "stars."

My vision returned to normal after a few seconds, and I jogged off to the sideline, with a big grin still affixed to my mug. Often it's the "hitter," not the "hittee," who gets the worst of a big hit. I couldn't have cared less. Monumental hits like that one are few and far between.

Cousineau went on to have a tremendous career at Ohio State. So great, in fact, that the Buffalo Bills made him the first pick in the NFL draft four years later. However, he opted to go north to Canada, where he played for the Montreal Alouettes for three years before making a return to the States and the NFL. I was there waiting for him.

I was drafted by the Detroit Lions the same year Cousineau was chosen and was still playing for them when he made his return to the NFL and the Cleveland Browns. Coincidentally, the Detroit Lions were slated to scrimmage the Browns at Bowling Green State University in Ohio that summer, and it would be Cousineau's first action against an NFL opponent. Fate, it seemed, was about to bring us together once again.

That scrimmage was also a proving ground for what would become two of the NFL's most successful coaches. A few of us on the Lions knew the Browns' new head coach, Marty Schottenheimer, quite well. He was previously employed as the Lions' linebacker coach, and there were still a few of us around that were on the team when he was a member of the Lions' staff. Longtime Pittsburgh Steelers coach Bill Cowher, who had not yet swapped his pads and helmet for a clipboard, was playing defensive back for the Browns that day.

If someone had told me I was going to experience the greatest hit of my life at Bowling Green, the career hit that I had been searching for ever since that cold, rainy day in Eastern Pennsylvania nearly a decade earlier, I would have told him he was crazy. But fortune often favors one when he least expects it.

Just as a surfer scours the coastline looking for that perfect wave, I had spent most of my football career searching for that perfect hit. I experienced some doozies, both on the giving and receiving end, in high school, college, and then the pros, but none had really measured up to the two I just described.

And that afternoon, in the middle of my fourth NFL summer camp, I have to admit I wasn't looking very hard. I had nothing to prove. My starting tackle spot was secure. I was tired and beat up from three weeks of two-a-days. I was looking forward to playing my slated couple of series, watching my teammates finish the scrimmage, and then getting the hell out of Ohio.

Cousineau might have been excited to play against his first live NFL competition, but I honestly couldn't have cared less at the time. At that point in my career, I wanted to use what was left of my body when it counted—during the regular season and the playoffs.

However, after whaling on my own teammates all summer, it was nice to go against some "fresh meat," as we called it. Still, it wasn't like it was the Super Bowl. On the ride down to Ohio from our training camp in Michigan, I told my linemates, all gritty NFL veterans, about the "shirt-off" incident from years before, trying to drum up some contrived enthusiasm for the scrimmage. They agreed to keep an eye out for him, but like me, their ebullience was lukewarm at best. But we all agreed we'd find some way to welcome Cousineau back to the United States, where the *real* football was played.

It was a hot, muggy afternoon, and I was already drenched in sweat after finishing our warm-up drills. I ran into coach Schottenheimer on the way back to our bench, and we briefly exchanged pleasantries. It was then that I noticed Cousineau for the first time, doing some stretching exercises behind Schottenheimer on the sidelines.

It was time to get down to business. Even though it was just a scrimmage, we knew we had to perform and do our job. Offensively, we would be expected to move the ball successfully against the Browns' first-string defense. The sooner our offense was productive, the sooner we would get pulled in favor of the guys struggling to make the team. To them, this scrimmage *was* the Super Bowl, and potentially the most important contest of their lives.

The scrimmage got off to a rather lackluster start. Both of the defenses dominated, while very little offense was generated on either side. Then, suddenly, everything changed.

Our offense finally had a drive going, and we moved the ball for the first time across midfield. A pass play was called. I was still blocking my man when I heard the "ball" call, which signaled an interception by the defense.

The perfect wave doesn't form unless wind speed, wind direction, swell, and tide all come together at precisely the right moment. The circumstances have to be just right. When searching the football field for that perfect hit, it's about foot speed, leverage, velocity, and the element of surprise. Both the perfect wave and the perfect hit depend mostly on luck and fate. I must have had plenty of luck that afternoon, and as far as fate goes, well, it was about to take a weird and bizarre turn.

I loved to tackle people. As I mentioned before, I was recruited to play defense at Penn State. But as an offensive tackle, my only opportunity to tackle someone was after an interception, and I took great pride in doing my best in those situations.

I came alive, shedding with my hands the defensive end I was blocking, becoming a defensive player once again. My strategy on an interception was simple. Find the ball and head straight for it, full speed ahead, rather than trying to figure out a pursuit angle. Initially, the interceptor was almost always looking down the field, searching for an opening, and waiting to pick up a block. I often was able to make the tackle before the interceptor had a chance to get going.

I was in a full sprint, running straight for the ball, when the ball carrier suddenly veered right in my direction. He was in a full sprint too, and I don't think he saw me until it was too late. This time I recognized who I was about to hit. At that point, though, it didn't make any difference. The collision was just a few milliseconds away. The irony of it all wouldn't register until later.

The impact was tremendous. Rob Rubick, a rookie teammate struggling to make the roster at the time, described it this way: "At that point, I was ready to pack up my gear and head back home, giving up my quest for a career in the NFL. It was one of the sickest sounds I've ever heard."

Luckily for the Lions, he stuck around and enjoyed a stellar seven-year career.

The shoulder pads I wore had one-inch-wide cloth strips running underneath each of my armpits, fastened to the front and back of the pads by metal rivets. The "unbreakable" strip of cloth running under my left armpit had ripped apart on impact.

Another supposedly unbreakable part of my protective armor, my face mask, broke on the play as well. The double bar running underneath my left eye bent down and in a good couple of inches, allowing some part of Cousineau's uniform, probably a shoulder pad blade, entrance to my face. It cut me just under my left eye and would later require 10 stitches to close.

The bottom buckles securing my four-way chin strap disintegrated on impact. My helmet, no longer secured to my head, smashed down hard on the bridge of my nose, splitting it open and sending blood flying everywhere.

Cousineau lay on the grass temporarily unconscious. I was on my hands and knees close by, also in Never-Never Land. A teammate told me later that even though the ball was free on the ground, the action stopped momentarily in deference to the hit, before a mad scramble for it ensued. We recovered the ball.

I got to my feet, still stunned from the impact but ecstatic nonetheless.

Ken Callicut, our star special-teams player and a big hitter in his own right, ran from the sideline and jumped on me in celebration. Laughing, he turned me around, and pointed in Cousineau's direction.

Cousineau got up, staggered toward us, then fell back down to the ground. He repeated this process a few times before some of his team-mates finally came to his aid, guiding him back to his side of the field.

I went back and got into our huddle. It was still our ball after the fumble recovery. It wasn't until then that I realized my shoulder pads and helmet and, for that matter, my face, were all broken. I wandered back to our sideline, searching out our equipment manager, but was met instead by my teammates, who treated me like I had just scored the winning touchdown in the Super Bowl.

From that point on, momentum was in our favor. Jerry Green, a sportswriter at the time for the *Detroit News*, had this to say in his column the next day: "It was the first time I ever saw a tackle on an interception single-handedly turn around a football game."

I can honestly look back on that play as the defining moment of my football career. Would I rather have had that moment occur at a more opportune time and place, like in the playoffs against the San Francisco 49ers at the "Stick," or against the Green Bay Packers at Lambeau Field? Or, for ultimate timing, in the fourth quarter of the Super Bowl? Of course. But you take what you can get, and I guess I'll have to settle for a meaningless scrimmage in Bowling Green, Ohio.

* * *

The Chicago Bears, during Mike Ditka's regime in the mid eighties, had some great football teams. Those teams were punctuated by a defensive unit many pundits call the best ever. Defensive coordinator Buddy Ryan used a tremendous lineup of athletes in a blitzing pres-sure scheme very few offenses could handle.

For nearly a decade, I battled twice a year against those guys, in particular future Hall of Famer Dan Hampton, the Bears' left defensive end, and Steve McMichael, their left tackle. Both were outstanding football players. On the other side of the line were Richard Dent and William the "Refrigerator" Perry.

The Fridge took up a lot of room, was a tough guy, and was a load against the run, but I relished the few times he would line up against me. After going up against McMichael and Hampton all those years, the Fridge always offered one constant. He was going to be there right in front of you when you came out of your stance to block him. With the other guys, who possessed tremendous quickness as well as strength, you weren't so sure.

Hampton got a lot of ink, and like I said, he's in the Hall of Fame, but I had the most respect for McMichael. No matter what I did to him, or what he would do to me, the man never uttered one single word to me on the field, and we played against each other nearly 20 times.

On one particular play, basically a student-body left with both guards pulling, my job was to simply clip him in the back of the knees. The play would immediately show away from me, to my left. McMichael lined up one player over from me, usually on the outside shoulder of the guard. Because the play showed so quickly to the left, and the man over him was pulling to the left and not blocking him, he would turn his shoulders and start running toward the ball. From my right tackle position, I would turn and bury my helmet right into the back of his knees, clipping him from behind. It was a cheap, dirty, unfair block but perfectly within the rules, and I took pride in doing it right.

The defensive tackles hated that block, because there was really not much they could do to defend against it; furthermore, any block that takes place around the knees is dangerous. Everyone knows a knee injury is one of the most prevalent and devastating injuries in football. I got in more fights over that block, but never with McMichael.

He'd just glare at me, get up, and try to take my head off on the next play. I respected that.

I was in Austin, Texas, during the off-season one year for a golf tournament, sitting in a local hangout, having a few cocktails with some friends when in walked McMichael. He walked over to me with this stern, intense look on his face. I honestly thought he was coming over to fight me. Instead, he shook my hand warmly and bought us both a shot of premium tequila. Like I said, I have the utmost respect for the man.

I'm sure McMichael and those other three got a big kick out of this next hit, especially the Fridge. I imagine they ran it back a few times in their own film room. Unlike the other hits I've described, I was on the receiving end, not the giving end, this time, and I have to admit it was a doozy.

We were playing the Bears at the Silverdome on *Monday Night Football*. We were trailing early in the fourth quarter but had a drive going, and I just knew we were going to score and make it a game. That's when I heard the "ball" call, signaling an interception.

Like so many times in the past, I came alive at the call, found the ball, and went right for it.

I learned early on that you need to "have your head on a swivel" during an interception, because those defensive guys would like nothing better than to take you out. It's the nature of the game. Very few athletes actually try to hurt anyone on purpose, but if it happens during a vicious, clean, and legal shot, so be it. To me, that's what football is all about. If you don't like it, find another game to play.

Quarterbacks know all about watching out for themselves during an interception. Next time you're watching an NFL game, check out the quarterback after he throws one. Most times he's going to have four or five 300-pound-plus dudes trying to kill him. It's quite comical really but, when you think about it, makes perfect sense. The quarterback is the most important player on the team, and is protected by the rules somewhat when he's in the pocket or scrambling; however, after he throws an interception, he's just another stiff who is as fair game as anyone. Of course you're going to try and get a shot in on him.

Yeah, I had my head on a swivel as I ran, but then I saw him. Their defensive back, who had made the interception, juked left, right, then left again, and now was running right at me, oblivious to my presence as he looked downfield for a block. I accelerated to my top speed (which isn't saying much), pumping my arms furiously as I ran, and was just about to knock this guy into the next county. That's when the lights went out.

When we watched the film the next day, I saw the Fridge was also running as fast as his 350-pound-plus body would take him. He lowered his head, dipping slightly right before catching me under the chin with his helmet. The back of my head was the first thing to hit the hard, unyielding Silverdome AstroTurf.

My teammates said the sound of our nearly 700 pounds of bulk colliding at full speed sounded like an explosion. I was told I got up, fell down, and then started toward the Bears' sideline before teammate Chris Dieterich grabbed me and led me back to our side. That's when my memory started to flicker back to normal. I had no idea what had happened or who had hit me—it had all happened so fast.

I was more embarrassed than anything, insisted I was all right, and played out the rest of the game. I did so in a fog, forgetting my assignment several times during the remaining quarter. There was once again a dull ache in my head for the next few days, and I guess I probably had suffered yet another concussion.

I remember my offensive line coach, Bill Muir, making a big deal out of the hit during our offensive line meeting. He waxed on and on about how we'd get back at that "big fat bastard" next year, and, as a unit, we weren't going to let him get away with it. I knew where he was coming from but felt very differently about the hit than he did.

I didn't particularly like any of those guys—they consistently kicked our asses during their glory years—but the Fridge was just playing football. Sure, I would relish doing the same to him someday, but I was more jealous than vindictive.

That hit *was* a real doozy.

Chapter 10

*%@$# Kickers!

"Hey, can I get you guys to stand over here, behind the bench, please?" Kent Falb, head trainer for the Detroit Lions, was forming a human shield around me. The injection I had gotten in my left hip at halftime hadn't helped much. They were going to try again, this time with more drugs and a bigger needle.

"And get that damn camera out of here!" he shouted.

Nothing like a big fat lineman's ass to help boost the television ratings.

The cold rain continued to come down. It had been raining steadily for the past 24 hours, and the field was a mess. Everyone—well, almost everyone—was completely covered in mud.

Candlestick Point, in San Francisco, California, sticks out into the cold Pacific Ocean, and the winter storms that stream down from the Gulf of Alaska hammer it ferociously with wind and rain. The players, or anyone else for that matter, didn't seem to mind. I looked around at the sea of red that blanketed the stadium, and there wasn't an empty seat in the house. They had been thoroughly entertained so far that afternoon, and the best was yet to come.

The noise was reaching a crescendo. The Detroit Lions' defense, which had played valiantly all afternoon, was

desperately trying to keep Joe Montana and his potent
49ers' offense out of the end zone. A field goal wouldn't
cut it for them. They needed six.

They had been held in check for most of the game but had come alive in the fourth quarter. Montana was rallying the troops. His pinpoint passing, despite the driving wind and rain, truly was a thing to behold.

It was New Year's Eve day, 1983, and the winner of the game would play next week for the NFC Championship and a chance to go to the Super Bowl.

The loser went home.

Every down I played as a Lion, every violent collision I endured, every wind sprint I ran, every off-season operation I stomached, I did so with one goal and one goal only in mind—to make it to the Super Bowl. This was our big chance. There was no way I was going to miss it.

"Let's get this thing done, Tweety. The defense is going to give us the ball back any second now," I pleaded. I was desperate. It was the fourth quarter of the biggest game of my life. We were up 23–17. I was determined to do whatever I could to help our team win. If I could just take the edge off this damn pain in my hip, I might be able to do my part. I strained to see over my teammates lining the sideline, cheering on our defense, which was desperately trying to get us the ball back.

I was violently kicked in the hip by my opponent for the day, Dwaine Board, back in the first quarter, and my "hip pointer" had progressively gotten worse. I considered myself lucky. It could have been worse—much worse. Just ask Steve Mott, our offensive center.

Nearly everyone, including myself, had replaced the front three spikes on their football shoes with longer, one-inch ones. This afforded us better traction out there in the quagmire that at one time had passed for a football field. Most of us would do anything for an edge up. Everyone was aware of the risk, including Steve, but he never hesitated.

One of the reasons injuries are so prevalent on AstroTurf is because the footing is *too* good. That's why most players prefer natural grass. The ground is more forgiving. When a hit is taken on your leg, grass will give way, allowing your foot to swing free, out of harm's way. The longer spikes gave us better traction on Candlestick Park's natural grass but negated this benefit. That's what happened to Steve. His spikes held firm in the mud, and we all knew by the obvious pain he was in—and the sickening angle of his leg—that he had suffered a serious knee injury. We would find out later that he had torn his anterior cruciate ligament in half. Steve was one tough cookie, though. He refused to stay in the locker room and was there on the sideline on crutches, cheering us on.

I watched our orthopedic surgeon, Dr. Robert Tiege, fill the syringe. First the Xylocaine, then the Novocaine. The "caine brothers," we called them. He flicked the syringe hard with his index finger several times, forcing the air bubbles to the top, then pushed the plunger upward until the pain-killing concoction squirted up through the long needle.

Our eyes locked. "Let's do it, Doc." I slid down my football pants to midthigh and pushed the elastic strap of my athletic supporter aside. He dug around with his fingers, eliciting a loud gasp from me with his third poke.

"Sorry," he said, as he took an isopropyl-soaked swab from Tweety, quickly cleansed the area, and then rammed the needle all the way home.

The caine brothers burned as they made their way deep into my hip. Just as the doc pulled the needle out, the crowd erupted. That couldn't be good. I finished doing up my pants, found my helmet, and rushed over to the sideline to watch the show.

I arrived in time to see Montana hit Freddie Solomon in the end zone for a touchdown. I remember looking into my fellow offensive linemen's eyes at that moment as we huddled together there on the sideline. No words were spoken. Even if they were, we wouldn't have been able to hear each other. The 49ers fans were going crazy.

We painfully watched the extra point sail through the uprights, which put the 49ers up by one.

Before I knew it, I was back in our offensive huddle. We had a long way to go and only about a minute left on the clock, but there wasn't a soul in that huddle who had any doubts that we were going to win this thing.

Billy Sims, who had gone over the 1,000-yard rushing mark for the third time earlier that season, had run his ass off all afternoon, gaining over 100 yards that day and scoring twice in the fourth quarter alone. Unfortunately, we couldn't afford to give him the ball anymore. We were going to have to milk the clock and get it downfield through the air.

Our quarterback, Gary Danielson, was brilliant. Just like his 49ers counterpart had done on their previous drive, he picked the defense apart with his pinpoint passing. Four completions later, we were all the way down on the 49ers' 25-yard line. There were only five seconds left on the clock. This was it.

It was going to be a 43-yard field goal, but our kicker had already hit a 53-yarder to end the half. It wasn't exactly a chip shot, but surely he could sail it through. A possible trip to the Super Bowl was at stake!

I will forever remember Eddie Murray's pristine uniform, clean and dry, as he stood there in the middle of our huddle. He stood out like a beacon, in stark contrast to the other 10 men, all of whom were literally covered with mud and soaked to the bone from head to toe.

I took my place on the line of scrimmage, confident of what I needed to do. A smile came over my face as I got down into my stance and looked inside at the ball. As soon as the ball disappeared, I stepped inside with my left foot, interlocking it with the foot of the guard next me, crying out in pain as I transferred my weight to the leg with the hip pointer. A surge of 49ers crashed into me, but I held firm, keeping my shoulders parallel to the line of scrimmage. Usually I can hear the sound of the kicker's foot hitting the ball, but the deafening crowd noise prevented me from hearing anything. I looked up after an appropriate interval and saw the ball sailing toward the uprights.

The next few moments appeared to transpire in super-slow motion and are captured in my memory forever, haunting me, teasing me, torturing me over and over again. From my angle, it appeared to be good, and I raised my arms into the air, a feeling of elation buoying my exhausted body. The pitch of the crowd, seemingly already at its maximum decibel level, erupted even louder as the ball sailed just wide right of the upright and careened harmlessly to the ground.

No good. My hands fell down to the top of my helmet in disbelief as the 49ers players in front of me celebrated wildly. Pandemonium ensued, temporarily overwhelming my senses. A sea of bodies enveloped me—jumping, screaming 49ers fans—all with arms flailing about wildly in celebration. It took me a moment to assimilate the drastic change of events. My elation turned to despair.

We had lost. No more postseason. No game next week. No Super Bowl. I stood there looking at the goal posts in disbelief, as tears welled up in my eyes. Fans jostled me about, oblivious to my sorrow, as they continued their wild celebration. I started to walk off the field and noticed that my hip felt the best it had all afternoon. Ironically, that last shot of the caine brothers had found its mark.

Later that night, and the whole next week, I would pay dearly for those shots. The deep bruise, which left me black and blue all the way down to my midthigh and upward to my stomach, was more serious than I had suspected. The following weekend I was still painfully limping around and, for a moment, wondered whether I would have been able to play if we had won. I immediately dismissed the notion. Of course I would have played. Some way, somehow, I would have found a way to get out there and do my job.

As it turned out, that was the closest I ever got to playing in a Super Bowl.

The drama for the day, however, wasn't yet over. As always after a game, win or lose, we wasted no time getting out of town. Just a few hours after our devastating loss, we were all packed onto our chartered stretch 727, taxiing down the runway at SFO.

Shortly after takeoff, we all knew something was seriously wrong. The plane banked severely as we were gaining altitude then leveled off abruptly. The captain announced that the plane had a mechanical problem and was dumping fuel into San Francisco Bay. We were going to make an emergency landing back at SFO. We were all instructed to assume emergency procedures, placing our heads between our legs— the whole nine yards. We landed safely, with fire trucks and emergency personnel at the ready, and ended up spending New Year's Eve in the nearly deserted international terminal. It was well after midnight when we got back in the air, and past dawn when we finally landed in Detroit.

During the plane ride home, a bunch of us gathered around a sleeping Eddie Murray, who was snoring away, lying across a row of three seats. Mike Fanning, a 12-year NFL veteran who played most of his career with the Los Angeles Rams, leaned his six-foot, seven-inch frame over the seats in front of him and had a little chat with the sound-asleep kicker.

Mike was quite the card. Earlier that year at a team Halloween party, he showed up with his wife, who was dressed in costume. Mike, on the other hand, was dressed in his usual attire—Wrangler jeans, cowboy boots, T-shirt, and baseball cap. Of course, the first question everyone asked him was where his costume was. He ignored the question, then after a few moments took off his hat, revealing a funny face painted on the front of his prematurely balding head.

"That's right, Eddie, you sleep. Sleep like you don't have a care in the world," he said in an exaggerated tone, as more players started to gather around.

"You know, Eddie, I want to thank you for missing that field goal today. Why? Well, I probably would've had one hell of a time figuring out how to spend that extra 15 grand, buddy," he said, as he started to spill a bit of his Coors beer onto the sleeping kicker's head. Besides the honor of advancing to the NFC Championship game, every player was due to make an extra $15,000 if we would have won, not a small sum given the salaries at the time.

I know this wasn't fair. Eddie was a heck of an NFL kicker. I'm sure he made way more winning field goals than he missed in his long and storied career. I'm sure he felt really bad about missing the one I just described. There's no doubt about it.

Danielson, who was the holder on field goals and extra points, told me the next day that Eddie's left foot, his plant foot, slipped in the mud, and that's why he missed. To this day, I wonder if things could have been different. Did Eddie replace the spikes on that shoe with longer ones like the rest of us had? Or, worse, was he wearing the rubber-cleated soccer shoes he normally wore when kicking on grass? Is there anything he could have done differently to have kept that foot from slipping?

I'm sure Eddie's off somewhere right now, calling me an obsessive, fat, bitter, ex-football player asshole and saying that I should get a life and to go fuck myself while I'm at it. I'm sure he's reminding himself that he made more money and played longer than I did. He's probably right. I deserve all that and more.

But it doesn't matter.

I still hate kickers.

That playoff game was the furthest I ever made it in the postseason. If he'd have sailed that field goal a few inches farther to the left, who knows what would have happened. We had a great defense. Our running attack was awesome, with a solid offensive line, and one of the best running backs, if not *the* best running back, of that era, Billy Sims, running behind us. We had a talented receiving corps, and a very underrated quarterback in Danielson.

Who knows what we could have done. A Super Bowl appearance, maybe even a victory, was a definite possibility. Given that success, the Lions might never have fired one of the best, if not *the* best, coaches in the league at the time, Monte Clark, and maybe I wouldn't have had to endure one humiliating losing season after another the rest of my career.

Maybe we would have made it to a *couple* of Super Bowls. And maybe my teammates and I would have made a few more Pro Bowls. And who knows, maybe the Hall of Fame.

Am I bitter? Damn right. Is this fair to poor Eddie? No. But damn it, I can't help it. I've moved on, I have a life, but I'd be lying if I said I don't think about that kick from time to time.

Is that why I hate kickers? Maybe. Or could it be that during the heat of summer, while I was beat up, sore, and miserable and running my umpteenth wind sprint and on the verge of passing out, I look over and see the kicker and the punter sitting on their helmets, jawing and laughing with each other, not a care in the world? Maybe I'm just jealous—jealous that I wasn't smart enough to choose a more sane position.

Or maybe it's because they're not really football players at all. What really irks me is when a "football player," for whatever reason, thinks he's above the game and not subject to the same dangers as everyone else. I remember Eddie throwing a hissy fit one time because someone blocked him on a kickoff.

Our opponent that Sunday must have noticed him keeping his head down after he kicked off, or maybe they just wanted to rattle him. Whatever the reason, just as the ball hit his foot, one of their guys, who had lined up the required 10 yards from the ball, ran right at him, hitting him under the chin, pummeling him to the turf, and opening up a gash on his face.

Well, I'd never seen anyone throw such a fit since my infant daughter lost her "binky" underneath the couch. There was no flag, no penalty—the hit was completely within the rules. As our special-teams coach tried to settle him down and our doctor checked out the cut on his face, a few of my linemates and I had to turn away and walk down to the other end of the sideline, our snickers growing into great big belly laughs.

Did he forget? It's a *football* game, for Christ's sake.

Kickers generally are different, a breed apart from your usual football player. I'm sure they think that's a good thing, and I'm cool with that.

Matt Bahr, our kicker at Penn State, took over the kicking duties from his brother Chris midway through my four years there. Both brothers went on to have long professional careers.

I remember I'd sit with Matt on a lot of our plane rides. He was friendly and intelligent, and we'd talk about all sorts of things other than football. It was apparent he had little interest in the sport other than kicking the ball, but I enjoyed the diversion. It helped relax me and calm my nerves somewhat.

Our travel arrangements always cracked us up. Penn State is in a very rural part of Pennsylvania and at the time was serviced by an airport that only allowed prop planes—no jets. We'd charter two large twin prop planes for most trips. I remember Matt and I would analyze the seating arrangements intently. We were convinced that Paterno and the other coaches meticulously went over the roster, placing a mixture of coaches, players, trainers, and equipment guys on each plane so that if one plane went down, the other plane would have a nucleus of personnel that would be able to carry on independently. We'd eagerly go over the plane assignments each week, checking the minute but meaningful changes (at least to us), trying to gain valuable insight into individual performance, based solely on which plane people were assigned.

For our longer road games, we'd bus down to Harrisburg so we could travel by jet. I remember one time I was sitting next to Matt, and he started to explain—in explicit detail—the engineering properties of our jet plane.

"Yes, Keith, if the engines on this airplane failed, we'd be in serious trouble, to say the least. The plane itself, without jet propulsion, actually possesses a negative drag coefficient, meaning that if the engines cut out, we wouldn't be able to glide to the nearest airfield to implement an emergency landing."

"You mean we'd crash?" I asked naïvely.

"What I'm saying is that we'd drop from the sky like a rock, the structure of the aircraft itself, without the aid of jet propulsion, providing absolutely no positive resistance to the wind. Worse, because of the ratio of the structural properties of the aluminum shell to the strong g-forces we would experience, the structure would actually break apart before we hit the ground."

"You mean we'd all die?"

"Precisely."

I tightened my seat belt and decided I needed to find a new travel partner.

A few years after I retired from the NFL, my former teammate and buddy Chris Dieterich came out to California for a visit. We decided to go see the Rams play the New York Giants at Anaheim Stadium. It would give us a chance to catch up with our old offensive line coach, Fred Hoaglin, who was now coaching for Bill Parcells' Giants in a similar capacity. I invited along my friend Mike Whelan, who I knew to be a rabid New York Giants fan.

We caught up with Fred after the game and were chatting amiably with him outside the tunnel where all the players come out. Mike was in heaven. Fred introduced us to all of the Giants players, and Mike had a chance to actually meet and talk to the players and coaches he idolized. That's when I spotted Matt, the Giants' kicker at the time.

I called him over, shook his hand, and asked how long had it been since we saw each other last—four years maybe? Didn't we run into each other after our game at the Meadowlands? I introduced him to Chris and Mike and expressed how good it was to see him again.

"I'm sorry, but who are you?" he asked me.

"Matt, you mean to tell me you don't remember me, your old teammate?"

"I'm sorry, but in my profession I meet a lot of people. Did you play for the Giants?"

Chris and Fred were laughing hysterically as I dismissed him rather rudely. I never did bother to tell him who I was. After my initial embarrassment, I started laughing as well. I noticed Mike had a rather disturbed look on his face.

"What the heck was that all about?" he asked.

"Don't worry about it, Mike," I explained. "That's a kicker for you."

Kickers continue to irritate me to this day, even in my retirement. While I was in the midst of writing this chapter, my alma mater, Penn State, was playing the University of Michigan at "The Big House" in Ann Arbor, Michigan. It was a regional television game, and my local television station was broadcasting a Pac-10 game. Thank goodness for my C-band satellite dish.

I clicked through the different bands, moving the big, 12-foot-diameter dish around the sky from my rural Northern California home. After about fifteen minutes of searching, there it was, on transponder G6, channel 24. I had found the ABC feed, broadcast without announcers, which was more than fine with me. The field mikes were on, so I could hear the players and the enormous crowd in all their glory. It was the first Saturday I'd had off in months, and my wife and kids were off doing errands. I grabbed myself a cold one and a box of some leftover spicy chicken wings from the fridge, settled into my favorite chair, and kicked off my shoes. My chores could wait.

The first thing I noticed, as the cameras showed Paterno prowling the sidelines, was that my old coach looked exactly the same as he did when I last played there nearly 25 years ago. How could that be? The last time I saw him in person, I had a full head of bushy, blond hair. I'm now in my mid forties, and I'm gray and balding. Paterno, on the other hand, even though he's in his mid *seventies*, appeared to have not changed a bit. I noticed his full head of thick black hair had only a touch of gray to it, as he nimbly paced back and forth, seemingly dictating every important decision as always. The man is timeless.

Penn State's notoriously boring away uniforms—all-white pants, white socks, black shoes, an all-white helmet with a single navy blue stripe down the middle, capped off with a white jersey with navy blue numbers and no name on the back—had changed, and to me this was startling. The last modification I could remember was my freshman year, way back in 1975, when our numbers were put on the side of our helmets. Joe deemed this as being way too fancy, though, and he promptly ordered the numbers removed.

But this year, in the two-inch-by-one-inch space between the face mask supports, right there on the front of the helmet, in teeny tiny lettering but clearly visible for the whole world to see, was the word "Lions." I was shocked. Joe *had* changed. He was obviously "gettin' jiggy wit it" in his old age.

It was a glorious game. The sun was shining, both teams were ranked in the top 20, and the crowd of 111,000-plus was going nuts. My beloved Nittany Lions played valiantly. Their defense fought mightily against a potent Michigan offense. The Penn State offense pulled off incredible play after incredible play, matching Michigan touchdown for touchdown.

But wouldn't you know it, Penn State's kicker missed two easy field goals and an extra point, and Penn State ended up losing in overtime.

It seems that I'm destined to have kickers haunt me for the rest of my life.

Chapter 11

Built Ford Tough

As I drove down Rotunda Drive, 222 Republic Avenue loomed monolithic in the distance, like some landlocked battleship with an enormous pitched roof. As I got closer, I saw it was not only a very aesthetically pleasing structure, fitting neatly into its surroundings, but the entire building was adorned with the Lions' Honolulu blue and silver colors.

Nice touch, I thought, as I maneuvered my rental car around the surrounding side roads, examining this magnificent facility from all angles, marveling at the size and scope of it. A warm sense of pride swam over me as I noted the Lions' logo, one of the coolest in the league, prominently displayed near the entrance.

It was quite a sight.

I was back in Detroit for the annual Detroit Lions Courage House award dinner. Every year since 1984, one player from each NFL team is selected as a recipient of the Ed Block Courage Award, and it is at this annual dinner that the Detroit Lions award winner is presented. The award is named after Ed Block, a longtime trainer for the Baltimore Colts who devoted much of his time and money to helping abused children, and the Detroit Lions created the Courage House to carry on his work in the Detroit area.

Through the generous sponsorship of the Detroit Lions, American Airlines, and others, I was a guest at the event this year, which happened to be held on my birthday in early December 2002. I have tried to attend every year since my retirement from the team, and hopefully will continue to do so for years to come.

The Detroit Lions Courage House provides support and resources for HAVEN, fashioned after the organization founded by Ed Block in Baltimore in 1989, and is part of the Courage House National Support Network. HAVEN, located in the city of Pontiac, is Oakland County's only comprehensive program for domestic-violence, sexual-assault, and child-abuse victims and their families. There are currently 15 such organizations around the country, all supported by the Network and a local NFL team.

My trip back to Detroit this year was even more special than usual. It was my opportunity to see brand-new Ford Field as well as the Lions' new offices and workout facilities, located on the border of Dearborn and Allen Park. I had come in a day early to make sure I was able to see it all.

The first thing that drew my attention was the parking. The players parked right next to the building, in an area reserved just for them! No 200-yard walk down a truck ramp like at the Silverdome. That alone was a tremendous improvement. Nothing, though, could have prepared me for what I was about to see inside.

I walked into the reception area. The ceiling reached far up to the heavens, the polished bamboo wood floor gleamed, and a collage of faces from the Lions' past stared back at me from the opposite wall.

"May I help you, sir?" the gothic-looking receptionist inquired.

"Keith Dorney to see Tim Pendell, please," I said, smiling widely. She wasn't impressed and studied me suspiciously as she buzzed Tim's office, which I imagined was somewhere beyond the 100-foot wall that rose up behind her. I had heard some bizarre stories of whackos trying to infiltrate the premises over the years. Did she think I was one of them? To be fair, I didn't look like a football player—or even an ex football player—anymore. She seemed surprised, and not necessarily pleased, that someone inside actually knew me, and I was told to have a seat.

I strolled around the lobby and noticed a door off to my right marked "Auditorium." I tried the door, but it was locked. This earned me a cold glare from the Goth, whose suspicious eyes had been following my meandering. I meekly retreated and sat down on one of the Honolulu blue–colored seats like I had been told.

There were still a lot of people with the Detroit Lions organization from my day, including Tim. He greeted me warmly, we exchanged pleasantries, and we began a leisurely tour of the facility.

It didn't take long for me to realize that things had changed—drastically. Old Gus, the ancient security guard at the Silverdome who always greeted me with a smile in the morning, apparently had lost his job. Tim placed his hand into a scanner, his finger-, thumb-, and palm prints were analyzed, and the bolt to the door electronically snapped open with a resounding "click."

Everything was brand-spanking-new, beautifully appointed, and thoughtfully laid out. It was obvious the Fords had spared no expense, and I couldn't imagine that a more functional, more aesthetically pleasing facility existed.

The media room had individual booths, each equipped with high-speed Internet access, and looked like something from the bridge of the starship *Enterprise*. Every group (offensive line, defensive line, running backs, and so on) on the team had its own individual meeting room. Media was no longer shown on 16-millimeter film, or even on videotape. One merely had to touch a button to project a football play onto the immense high-definition screen. Want to show last week's game? Or next week's opponent's game from three weeks ago? How about all draw plays run by your opponent in their last three games, or every "Flow 38" run by your offense since the beginning of the season? No problem. Push a few buttons and it's downloaded from a massive networked hard disk somewhere in the building and transferred onto your screen via some ultramodern fiber-optic cable behind the wall with the bandwidth capacity of the Alaskan pipeline.

I embraced my good friend Mark Glenn, now the head equipment manager, upon entering the locker room. After a quick tour, he proudly guided me back, way back, into the inner depths of the equipment room.

"Check it out, Cheese, just like old times." There, amongst the shelves and aisles of equipment, were two dilapidated but comfortable recliners and a beat-up coffee table. During my entire tour, these were the only pieces of furniture or equipment I recognized from the old facility.

"Ah, just like I remember it," I said, as I sat down on my favorite chair. Often, we'd spend time away from the hustle and bustle of the locker room, deep in the interior of the Silverdome, the loud industrial-sized dryers masking all sounds, and just relax, drink coffee, and sit around and bullshit.

"I miss you, Cheese," he said, and I could see from Mark's face that somehow things weren't the same. I wondered if any of the current players sat with him back here. Did they take him out for a beer after practice on Thursdays like I and the rest of the offensive line used to do? Somehow I doubted it. It's their loss. Mark is a heck of a guy and will always be my good friend, even though I don't see him very much these days.

"The Big Cheese returns," Joe Recknagel announced, as we made our way into the training room. I gave him a big bear hug. Joe must have taped my ankles a thousand times.

He showed me around the futuristic training room. There was a wing filled with sophisticated-looking rehabilitation equipment. A separate area contained jogging, hydrotherapy, and conditioning pools. Still another sector was dedicated to readying the players for practices and games, with cleverly engineered taping tables and benches.

It was a far cry from the stark stainless-steel whirlpool tubs and a couple of rolls of tape that I remembered from the old training room.

Tim held open the locker room door for me, and we exited into a hallway, continuing the tour.

"Tim, were you able to set up that meeting with Mr. Ford?" I inquired hopefully.

I had been talking to Tim for weeks about this coming trip and was hoping to spend a few minutes with William Clay Ford Jr., the vice chairman of the Detroit Lions and chairman of the board and CEO of Ford Motor Company. Along with his dad, William Clay Ford, they run the Lions, and also own a good chunk of Ford Motor Company. I wanted to talk to him about not only the future of the Detroit Lions but his role as head of Ford Motor Company as well.

We are around the same age, and I vividly remember when we first met. Both of us were nervous, wide-eyed youngsters, walking around the locker room before an early-season game. I was a rookie with the team, he was an undergraduate at Yale University, and I remember thinking we were sort of in the same boat, give or take a few hundred million dollars.

"My book could really use some perspective from management's side of things," I explained. "Plus," I joked nervously, "I was going to see if I could finagle a new paint job for my Ford pickup."

"Keith, I know he wanted to meet with you, but he's just too darn busy with board meetings and the like this week. He's working real hard, fulfilling his duties with both the Lions and Ford Motor Company."

I said nothing, trying not to show my disappointment and embarrassment.

I personally know a little about Fords and a little about football, so the hell with it, I decided. I'm going to lend my own commentary on the subjects with or without the interview.

I've had only a handful of vehicles in my day, and two of them have been Ford trucks. The first one was my Econoline, which I bought with my bonus money when I was a rookie.

My old dog Boss—who has long since passed after a happy life—myself, and a colorful cast of constantly changing driving companions, drove that sucker across the country *18* different times, and every one of them was an adventure to remember. It was almost three hundred thousand miles later when I finally got rid of it. It had needed a new transmission, and I hadn't felt like dealing with it at the time, so I sold it to the owner of the Aamco transmission shop in Capistrano Beach, California, back in 1988.

I regret that decision to this day. It was still running well on the original straight-six 300-cubic-inch engine, and the body was in impeccable shape. I feel now like I abandoned an old friend.

I won't make the same mistake again. I currently own a 1989 Ford F150 pickup, which I also bought new, and I plan to keep it forever. And why not? It's just getting broken in, with a little over two hundred thousand miles on it and the original 302 V-8 engine still purring like a kitten (with the addition of my Flowmaster exhaust system, it actually roars more like a lion). With two kids and two dogs, it really comes in handy. I'm going to let my son, Clayton, have it when he turns 16 in a couple of years. Then, it's my daughter, Alea's, turn to drive it. After they both have earned enough money to buy their own Fords, I plan to re-inherit it and drive it for the rest of my life.

Now, what about the football side of things? In 2001 the Lions were a dismal 2–14, matching their worst record ever, which occurred back in 1979, my rookie year. And 2002 wasn't turning out to be much better. The last time the Lions won a championship was the year I was born. It's been way too long. Things have got to change.

I'm the first to admit that I'm way more objective talking about Ford trucks than I am about what is ailing the Lions. It's not that I'm not qualified. I had spent a decade with the team—from 1979 to 1988—when I retired, and saw quite a bit in my years with the organization and still keep close tabs on them. The problem is that I still bleed Honolulu blue and silver, the Lions' official colors, and I'm the first to admit I'm more than a little prejudiced. No one wants to see the Lions play in a Super Bowl more than I do.

Still, I was determined to find an answer, with or without that interview, and planned to keep my eyes and ears open.

Seemingly appearing out of nowhere, there we were, standing on a football field—an exact replica of the one at Ford Field, I was told—complete with sidelines, goal posts, and a ceiling that was over 100 feet high. The surface was covered with FieldTurf, that futuristic, state-of-the-art artificial turf I'm told the players love.

I couldn't resist. I took a few steps and dove onto the surface, landing on my good shoulder, and executed a little somersault, much to the delight of my tour guide, Tim. It was soft, forgiving, and ever so cushy.

"Cheese, you could have played three more years if we'd had this stuff back in your day," Tim commented, as I rolled around on it like some big kid in a new, giant-sized playpen.

My career was ended by an arthritic left knee that endured too many hours of play on the rock-hard surface of the Silverdome. Ironically, that knee now buckled slightly then cracked loudly as I picked myself up off the surface.

At that moment, I couldn't help but think of my good friend and former teammate Chris Dieterich. I had gotten an e-mail from him the week before this trip, telling me he was scheduled to get a titanium hip replacement in early 2003.

Tim and I walked down to the far end of the field, where a bevy of massage therapists had their tables set up in one corner. They were working on several players as well as an older, overweight gentleman I assumed was on the coaching staff.

"You've got to be kidding me," I commented, shaking my head, eliciting a big smile from Tim.

"Cheese, massage therapy is a legitimate science these days, as you probably know, and we're trying to do whatever possible to help the health of our players."

"I was born too early," I thought out loud, as we continued the tour. The next stop was the weight room.

The old weight room, although well equipped for its time, was windowless, smelly, and dusty, located deep inside the bowels of the Silverdome, down yet another truck ramp from the locker room. This one was multilevel, four times as big as the old one, and equipped with an incredible array of machines and free weights.

Windows reached from top to bottom of the cavernous room, letting in generous amounts of natural light, such a contrast from the dungeons in which I had grown accustomed to working out.

Again, I didn't recognize a single piece of equipment from the old facility. Everything was brand-spanking-new—and spotless. I was like a kid in a candy store as I walked around, checking out what has to be one of the premier workout facilities in the world.

Tim announced it was time for lunch.

The next few minutes left me breathless, unbelieving, and stupefied. Everything I had just seen, however wonderful, futuristic, and first-class, was simply the cake. What I witnessed next was the icing, with cherries and extra sprinkles on top.

As I toured the dining room, I met the players' personal chef and watched as a cadre of kitchen workers prepared the afternoon meal for the players and staff. Fresh, lean, beautiful chicken fillets were being lovingly sautéed in a white cream sauce, the aroma smelling of freshly chopped garlic and onion. Fresh vegetables were being sliced and diced. Atop an industrial-sized stove, homemade chicken noodle soup simmered in a big pot, from which emanated smells that would make Wolfgang Puck salivate.

Along the food line, there were real eating utensils, not plastic, from which to choose. An array of gourmet desserts, yogurts, energy drinks, and fresh fruit cocktails were laid out on ice. Every item was labeled, describing it along with calorie content and nutritional information. There was a big bowl of salad greens. They were *real* greens, not just iceberg lettuce, with endive, bib, oak leaf, romaine, and bits of arugula thrown in for flavor. Spending as much time in Detroit during the winter as I had, I knew that stuff wasn't easy to come by.

"Cheese, the players are served both breakfast and lunch—at no charge—every day that they're here."

"No, you're kidding me, right?" I asked, awestruck, as my jaw dropped in amazement.

Tim just shook his head, smiling. He was serious.

"You remember back when I was playing, right? It was a big deal when we finally convinced management to let us send Mark Glenn out for Popeye's chicken on Thursdays, at *our* cost, of course."

And that was just one meal. The rest of the time we were on our own. In my later years, with the help of my wife, I brown-bagged it. When I was a bachelor, I didn't eat so well during the day. I usually didn't have enough foresight, or energy, to pack a lunch.

"Oh, I remember," Tim replied, smiling. "We used to be able to smell that chicken up in the offices upstairs. It permeated up through the ceiling. I can still smell it to this day."

"Yeah, we'd order something like 200 pieces of chicken. That's a lot of chicken."

"The lunch of champions," Tim added.

"I'm not sure of the nutritional value," I countered. "And at the time I don't think I really cared, but it did wonders for morale, and as I recall, that was some pretty doggone tasty chicken. *Love that chicken from Popeye's,*" I sang badly. "That's got to be something you miss about Pontiac. I doubt there's another town in the United States with three chicken joints kitty-corner from each other—Kentucky Fried Chicken, Church's, and Popeye's. Although, with a setup like this, I guess you guys don't eat out much, do you?"

My chicken rant was suddenly interrupted. Big hands grabbed me from behind by the shoulders.

"Hoofenglauffer," Matt Millen whispered in my ear. I stood up and embraced my old friend warmly. The last time we had seen each other we were beating the living crap out of each other at the Coliseum in

Los Angeles, California. That was way back in 1987, when Matt played for the Oakland Raiders.

And now, here he was, dressed like a preacher, president and general manager of the Detroit freakin' Lions. It was great to see him.

Ever since 1972 we'd competed against each other on the football field. Our respective high schools, Emmaus and Whitehall High, located in the Lehigh Valley of Eastern Pennsylvania, used to play each other on Thanksgiving Day. I was a year older than Matt, and he followed me to Penn State, where we again competed against each other, this time every day in practice.

Then it was on to the NFL for both of us, where our fierce rivalry continued. We played against each other several times in the pros, but up until that last meeting, it was Howie Long who lined up on my nose, not Matt. That last game, however, I was playing guard, not tackle, and Matt and I once again were nose to nose with each other on every play, just like old times.

Right from the start, I knew it was going to be unlike any game I had ever played. I remember that first play. I was especially geeked and came off the ball hard, unloading on him with everything I had.

"Holy cow, Hoof, nice hit. I'm going to have to give that one to you. You knocked me back a couple of yards," Matt said with a wide grin, patting me on the ass as we disentangled ourselves from each other. The rest of the game, after practically every single play, he'd grade our performance.

"I think I got the best of you that play, Hoof. I stoned you right on the line of scrimmage." Or "Heck of a hit, big guy, but you didn't keep your feet. I'm calling this one a draw."

"Hoof," short for "Hoofenglauffer," was my nickname in college, at least to Matt, Frank Case, and a few other of my Eastern Pennsylvania teammates who got the joke. It was a play on all the funny-sounding Pennsylvania Dutch names that proliferated on my high school's roster—names like Kopenhaver, Schantzenbach, Lichtenwalner, and Knappenberger.

In between plays, he'd be hollering and carrying on conversations with my teammates, insulting our quarterback, and calling our left guard a "fat ass."

I remember Rich Strenger, who was playing tackle next to me, asking, "What the hell is up with that No. 55? That guy is *crazy!*"

Yes, he was crazy. Late in the fourth quarter, with the outcome of the game still very much in question, right before the most crucial play of the game, he came up to the line, got in my face, and started yelling, "This is it, Dorney, right here and now. Hokendauqua versus Macungie, Hokendauqua versus Macungie!" (referring to our Pennsylvania hometowns).

Bill Keenist joined us at the lunch table. He was another holdover from my time and was now a senior vice president. A few minutes later, head coach Marty Mornhinweg joined us as well.

A bunch of guys in suits, none of whom I recognized, walked into the room, got their lunches, and sat down at the opposite end of the room from us.

"Who are those guys?" I inquired.

"Ford people," Matt answered and changed the subject.

As I chatted with coach Mornhinweg, a television off to the side of the room but in full view suddenly flashed his name and face up on the screen. All eyes and attention shifted to the screen. The sound was off, but it was closed-captioned and tuned to some talk show on an all-news network.

A couple of talking heads were debating a variety of topics, each limited to a minute of discussion. Marty's decision to take the wind—not the ball—after winning the coin toss at the start of the Lions' overtime period versus the Chicago Bears the previous week was the topic on the table. Should Mornhinweg have gone with the odds and taken the ball? Marty's gamble had backfired. The Bears had taken the kickoff and marched right down the field to score, ending the game and handing the Lions their eighth loss in eleven tries.

We all watched the debate, which wasn't exactly supportive of his decision. Coach Mornhinweg shrugged his shoulders and turned his attention back to me.

"Keith, the conditions in that stadium were such that every single score in the game came when the offense had the wind. Our defense was playing well. At the time it seemed like the thing to do."

I nodded my head as Matt put in his two cents.

"There were probably 80 critical decisions he had to make during that game, all of them crucial to the game's outcome. That was just one of many. Why all the focus on it? It was a well-informed decision that could have just as easily won the game for us."

Matt obviously supported the coach's decision to relinquish the ball to the Bears, despite the fact that over 70 percent of overtime games played in the NFL are won by the team that gets the ball first. It was a gutsy call, but given the circumstances, who knows, I might have done the same thing. It's so easy to second-guess. They were in a tough spot, with an incredibly tough job, and I didn't envy their positions one bit.

After lunch, Matt and I retreated to his office. We holed up in there for most of the rest of the afternoon, catching up on news about our kids, our wives, our families. It wasn't until then that I realized how much Matt meant to me. We had so much history together, had so much in common, but spent most of our lives competing head-to-head. Sitting there in his office, after all those years and years of fierce competition, I realized that the man was my good friend, not my enemy. I told him so.

The competition was over.

We talked about old college teammates. Guys like Bruce Clark, Kip Vernaglia, Mike Guman, Chuck Fusina, and Tom Donovan.

We talked about the last football game we played in as teammates, the 1979 Sugar Bowl, when Penn State played Alabama for the National Championship. In the course of doing research for this book, I had watched a tape of that game the previous week—for the very first time—and it was still fresh in my brain.

"Matt, I know it was a long time ago, but you had a hell of a game that night. You made a lot of plays."

"Funny you mention that. My kids were watching a replay of that game on *ESPN Classics* not too long ago, and all I heard from the other room was: "Hey, Dad, you just missed another tackle!""

We both laughed hard.

To my surprise, Matt brought up the name of Jerry Wenner, a teammate of mine from Emmaus High School.

"Yeah, that Jerry Wenner, he could really bring it!"

"Matt, Jerry's a year older than *me*. The last time you played against him was Thanksgiving Day, *1973*. That's almost 30 years ago!"

"Like I said, the guy could bring it."

Our laughter again filled the room.

"So, how are your folks?" I asked tentatively, knowing they must be getting up there in years.

"They're doing great." He told me both his mom and dad were now in their eighties, healthy, and doing well. He filled me in on the particulars.

I told him of my mother's passing.

"I miss her so much," I started to explain. I started to get teary eyed, so I quickly changed the subject. "I'll never forget that golabki your mom used to make for me. She still make it?"

"You bet. And she taught Patricia [Matt's wife] how to make it, too."

"Ah, you're a lucky man."

While in college, Matt would often catch a ride with me for a visit back home. Matt's mother, grateful for the opportunity to see her son, showed her appreciation to me by baking me huge trays of golabki, a Polish delicacy, for me to take back to the dorm.

"Man, that was some good golabki."

"Yep."

OK. Enough with the stuffed cabbage talk. It was time to start asking the tough questions.

"So, Matt, what's the problem? Why can't the Lions win? Are they going to let you hang around long enough to get the job done?"

There. I'd said it. After three hours, I'd managed, in five seconds, to blurt it out. It's not like he hadn't been asked this same thing before. Reading the sports pages, listening to the talk radio programs the last few days, and occasionally checking up on my boys from my computer at freep.com, the web site for the *Detroit Free Press*, I knew the local media was all over him.

He pondered the questions, looked me right in the eye, and spoke.

"Keith, you've been with this organization a lot longer than I have. What do you think the problem is?"

Tricky bastard, I thought. Well, if I showed him mine, maybe he'd show me his.

"Matt, I've been away a long time. Things have changed a lot since I last played here. All I can do is reflect on what I perceived as the problem when I was here. Let me tell you a story that I think best illustrates what I'm talking about. If I do that, then I want you to share *your* thoughts with me. OK?"

"Sure."

"My contract was going to expire at the end of the season, and Russ Thomas, the general manager at the time, called me up into his office. I was up there for a good two hours, and he never brought up my contract once."

"What did you talk about?"

"Except for a few minutes of pleasantries, he mostly quizzed me about head coach Monte Clark. He wanted to know what coach Clark said about him in the team meetings. He wanted to know what coach Clark said about him to me privately. He wanted to know what I thought coach Clark felt about him. He wanted to know if coach Clark made any remarks about him while he was taking a piss in the next urinal over from mine. Every time I tried to bring up my contract, he'd steer the conversation back to Monte this, Monte that. Monte, Monte, Monte."

"Did you know that I've got Monte working with us right now? He was in here earlier today. Great guy. Really knows his football."

"Yes, I heard," I said. "I'm disappointed I didn't get a chance to see him. Kudos to you for using him as a resource. Monte was—is—a great coach. I've always thought the world of him."

"Nine and seven is looking pretty good right now," Matt added, laughing, referring to Monte's best record as the Detroit Lions' head coach, which he achieved twice during his seven-year reign. Up to that point in the 2002 season, Matt's record with the Lions was a dismal 5–23 (the Lions ended up dropping their remaining four games in 2002, making that mark 5–27).

I sympathized with his position. I knew it only too well as a player. Matt, on the other hand, was new to this kind of misery. When we were teammates in college, 10–2 was considered a disappointing season (my last two seasons at Penn State, we went 22–2). During his professional playing career, he couldn't have been more successful, winning an incredible four Super Bowls with three different teams.

"Anyway, let me get back to my story. So I leave Russ' office, and I don't get halfway down the hallway, and Monte grabs me, takes me into his office, shuts the door, and wants to know what Russ said about him!"

"That's what was wrong," I continued. "Too many factions. Too many 'groups.' Too much corporate bullshit. This organization needs everyone on the same page, everyone pulling as one, everyone doing whatever it takes to produce a winner. Anyone in this organization who isn't trying to help the team win on Sunday—from the person who answers the phone to the guy who signs the checks to the one who sorts the fucking jockstraps—should be outta here."

Matt pondered my words for a moment before responding.

"Keith, after a short period of acclimation and getting to know everyone, I instituted some serious changes here.

"First off, I made some personnel moves across the board—staff, administration, and players." He rattled off a bevy of names, some of whom I recognized, others whom I did not.

I nodded my head in agreement. One particular individual, a racist son of a bitch if I ever did meet one, was let go by Matt soon after his arrival. I thought it extremely perceptive of Matt—rooting that person out as quickly as he did—and was generally very impressed with the moves he had made.

"That must have caused quite a stink," I said, stating the obvious.

"Yes, initially it did, but it had to be done. I was given complete control of football operations when I signed on here. Otherwise I wouldn't have taken the job. Anybody I thought was here for any other reason than to try to help us win football games—which, like you said, should be the ultimate goal of everyone in this building—I let go."

Matt paused. I shook my head in admiration.

"I also reorganized our compensation policy for administration and staff. The Fords have always been quite generous with year-end bonuses. I didn't change that, but I did tie it to winning football games. The more we win, the more everyone benefits."

"Not too much bonus money being thrown around these days, huh Matt?"

"Dorney, you always were a smart ass."

"Matt, all I've heard since I got here is how it's not like it used to be when we played. Specifically, that guys are too worried about their contracts, too worried about the almighty buck, to do the things you have to do when you play in the NFL. Do you find that to be true?"

"Well, Hoof, the salary cap definitely changed everything. When we played, if you didn't do your job—poof, you were gone. When I first arrived and began evaluating this team, it was obvious to me and others that we had some players who simply couldn't play. But, because of that damn cap, we had to keep them. That drove me crazy. Thankfully, we have gotten rid of those players over the past few seasons.

"This job can be very frustrating at times. But I do want to finish what I started here . . ."

His voice trailed off.

It was getting late. Both of us had to get ready for the Ed Block Courage Award dinner, which was being held downtown at Ford Field. I was really looking forward to the event and my first opportunity to see the facility I had heard so much about.

I was literally out the door, on my way back to the hotel, when I turned back around. There was one other person I needed to see. I approached the receptionist. The Goth had been replaced by a pretty, pleasant young woman, who smiled at me when I asked to see Russ Bolinger. She picked up the phone and pushed a few buttons.

"Keith Dorney to see you, Mr. Bolinger."

Thirty seconds later, we both heard muted screaming down the upper corridor, then it started to get louder—and louder. The receptionist looked over at me with horror in her eyes. Did some 350-pound lineman flip out after getting put on waivers and start rampaging through the hallways? As the yelling got closer, I recognized its source. A smile came across my face, then I started laughing out loud, putting the receptionist at least a little bit at ease.

A smiling Bolinger appeared at the top railing.

"Hey, Dorney, come off the ball, you know what I mean!"

"Boli!" I yelled in return.

He disappeared from the top railing and reappeared a few seconds later downstairs. We grabbed each other, wrestled around, and embraced. It had been years since we had seen each other.

Boli and I comprised the right side of the Detroit Lions' offensive line for years and years. He played right guard; I played right tackle.

Our relationship did *not* get off to a good start. Boli was four years my senior, and back when I was a rookie, in 1979, rookies were expected to work hard, keep their mouth shut, and take whatever shit was thrown at them.

During my first summer camp, near the end of a long, hard morning practice, I started messing around with Boli, thinking I was starting to get accepted as "one of the boys." It was way too soon. I had overstepped an invisible boundary that separated veteran players from rookie scum. Something I said was misinterpreted, and before I knew what had happened, he had sucker punched me in the mouth, knocking out one of my front teeth.

"Fuck you, you cocky-ass rookie!" I remember him screaming at me, as a bunch of his fellow veterans restrained me. After finally figuring out what had happened, I was burning mad and wanted nothing better than to tear his head off.

My anger grew and grew, and I made a vain attempt at revenge in the locker room after practice, only to be restrained once again by a group of veterans watching his backside.

Monte Clark was especially upset at the tiff that had developed between us. He called me into his office and explained that he had planned to promote both me and Russ into the starting lineup the very next week.

"How can I have my two starting linemen on the right side of my line hating each other? Maybe this isn't such a good idea."

I wanted that starting job more than a front tooth, or even revenge. Monte made me solemnly swear there would be no further retaliation.

"No problem," I immediately promised. I would have agreed to just about anything at that moment. I was going to be the Lions' starting right tackle!

"Shoot, Dorney, for that next month, I just knew your big ass was going to come out of nowhere and punch me in the mouth," Boli later confided in me.

That never happened. We were the right side of the Detroit Lions' offensive line for the next four years, opening up holes for the likes of Dexter Bussey and Billy Sims, protecting our quarterbacks Gary Danielson and Eric Hipple, and kicking some serious ass.

He helped teach me how to be tough and how to play with pain. I remember one particular incident during that first year. It was late in the season. Our record was abysmal, but Boli and I had held firm all year, side by side, never giving up, defending whatever quarterback lined up behind us, scratching and battling every play, no matter what the score. We were playing the Green Bay Packers, and I had just gotten my thumb caught between my helmet and the helmet of one of their linebackers as we violently collided. I came back to the huddle moaning. Blood was oozing from both the nail and a big gash on the knuckle, and it hurt like hell. I looked toward the bench. Boli grabbed me by the face mask with both of his hands and put his face inches from my own.

"You're not going anywhere, Dorney. I need you right here. We've played every fucking play together this whole, miserable, goddamn year, and you're not going to bail out on me now, you hear me? At the end of this series, you can put some tape on it or get the fucking thing cut off, but you're not leaving this field!"

Thanks in large part to Boli, I played every down at tackle that year. We became good friends. I owe Boli another debt of gratitude as well. He's the guy who invited me to come stay and work out with him in California that first off-season. If he hadn't done that, I never would have spent my off-seasons in California, or met the love of my life—my wife Katherine—and my two wonderful children never would have been conceived.

Boli was now head of collegiate scouting for the Lions. He downplayed his important role with the organization as he showed me his end of the building.

"Yeah, Dorney, ya see here, this is the nerve center of the scouting operation. You come back off the long road trip, you've got your coffee, your microwave popcorn, and all the bottled water you can drink."

Boli, one of the funniest guys I've ever known, had me in stitches most of our visit. I asked him how he got along with Matt Millen.

"Let me tell you, Dorney, the first time I talked to him, I'm thinking my ass is fired for sure. I met him in the hallway, and Matt, he goes to me: 'Yeah, Bolinger, I remember you. You're the guy who would never hit me up high, the guy that was always cutting me down at the knees.' So I tell him, what was it you wanted me to do? I see your big, fat, 280-pound ass running at me, *of course* I'm going to cut you!"

I'm on the floor, I'm laughing so hard.

"And he got pissed! Didn't think what I said was funny at all. But to his credit, he didn't take it personally, and luckily I still have a job."

As I had with Matt a short while before, we brought each other up-to-date on some of our old teammates. He told me our old lifting buddy, Steve Riley, who played a dozen years for the Minnesota Vikings, was on total disability and could barely walk. A few months earlier, Boli continued, he had visited with our old quarterback, Eric Hipple—in jail—where he had ended up following a downward spiral after the suicide of his son.

I was particularly devastated at that news. I love Eric Hipple. We had been through so much. We owned a boat together at one point in our lives and had shared many a good time both on and off the field. And he was the toughest damn quarterback I had ever been around.

We shared stories of other long-lost teammates. Boli brought up the name Rick "Kano" Kane. He was one of my favorite players on the team. Rick and his wife, Jan, had always treated me well. He was a great guy, tough, and one hell of a running back.

"Boli, I'll never forget my first halftime. You probably don't remember the game, but I sure do. It was my first NFL game. Against the Bills in Buffalo. I'm sitting there next to Rick, and he lights up a cigarette! I couldn't believe it. I thought he was completely off his rocker. We just didn't do that at Penn State, if you know what I mean. Then I see Monte Clark stomping over to us, and I'm thinking Rick's in some serious shit. Boy, was I surprised when Monte bummed a smoke off him."

We both laughed hard.

My Rick Kane memories came pouring out. I probably hadn't thought of him, much less mentioned his name, in years.

"Do you remember the time we were playing the Packers in Milwaukee?"

My rookie year, Green Bay was still playing half their games at Lambeau Field and half at Brewer Stadium.

"Remember how both teams shared the same sideline there? I think that was the only game I ever played, at any level, where both teams were on the same side."

Boli smiled, nodding his head, obviously reveling in my sudden recollections and enthusiasm.

"The offense is running off the field, and some little defensive back from Green Bay is running his mouth at us, calling us every name in the book. I run by him, thinking to myself how someone should do something about that asshole. Then I hear this commotion behind me. I turn and there's Kano, on top of this guy, just pummeling the shit out of him!"

We laughed hard once again, Boli just barely able to utter "of course I remember" through his big belly laughs.

There was more good news, but a large majority of it was very sad. We talked of hip and knee replacements, divorce, and financial ruin. We spoke, with reverence and respect, of our former teammates John "Woody" Woodcock and Steve Furness, both of whom have passed. It reminded us both of the harsh realities of the tough and brutal sport that we both once played and the toll it can take on one's life.

"Chris Dieterich is going under the knife early next year. Getting a new hip put into him."

Boli nodded, grimacing in commiseration.

"You remember Irv Pankey?" I went on.

Boli nodded. "Hell yes!"

Irv was a teammate and good friend of mine from Penn State, and Boli knew him from his days with the Los Angeles Rams.

"He just got his second titanium hip put in earlier this year."

We looked into each other's eyes. We knew, without words, that we were two of the lucky ones.

Mostly, though, we remembered the good times. We talked about our old offensive linemates Karl "Big Hoss" Baldischwiler, Homer Elias, and Amos Fowler. We reminisced about football games played long ago, about fishing trips on Lake Huron, about our road trip to his hometown of Lompoc, California, for a barbecue and charity basketball game. And we laughed and laughed and laughed.

By the time I finally pulled myself away, threw on my suit back at my hotel room, and drove downtown to Ford Field, I was horribly late.

I nearly missed my exit off of I-75. Ford Field fit into the downtown landscape like a glove. No small task making a sixty-five-thousand-seat arena blend into its surroundings. The Fords once again had done it up right.

After gaining entry, I immediately started to roam about, forgetting about being late. I couldn't help myself. It was beautiful.

I wandered down an aisle and sat down in one of the seats. I could see the Renaissance Center tower and the surrounding downtown buildings through the glass windows at one end of the stadium. I spied the solid-brick wall comprising the facade opposite me, which was part of the historic Hudson warehouse that had been incorporated into the new construction. I looked up and marveled at the enormous steel trusses that supported the gigantic roof.

Unlike the sterile, generic Pontiac Silverdome, this place was uniquely Detroit. The stadium was awash in the Lions' colors. The Lions' logo, just like at the practice facility, was visible everywhere.

Never had I seen a more aesthetically pleasing, more intimate setting for football than the one that lay before me. I wanted to suit up, to play there down on the soft FieldTurf, and to hear the crowd roar once again.

I imagined this glorious stadium filled to the rafters, the national anthem being belted out by Aretha Franklin, and No. 70 standing down there on the sideline at attention, taped, padded, and adorned in all my regalia, ready to do battle for my team.

Back when I played, the national anthem was always a good time for me to reflect on how fortunate—and what an honor—it was to be playing for the Detroit Lions. I remembered how grateful I was simply to be standing there on the sideline before an NFL football game, at Veteran's, Lambeau, Mile High, Three Rivers, the "Stick," the "Murph," the "Big Sombrero," or even the goddamn Pontiac Silverdome.

The tingling started slowly, low and deep inside me, and then suddenly started shooting up my spine, reaching a crescendo as I imagined Aretha singing that last verse of our national anthem—*and the land of the free . . .*—and the crowd standing and roaring its approval.

I wanted to play for the Lions again, in the greatest football stadium I had ever seen, and win that championship for them—for me. As often happened when I would hear those last sweet words of our anthem, tears began welling up in my eyes then falling down my cheeks. I leaned forward so as not to stain my suit pants.

"Um, sir, I'm sorry, but you're not allowed down here. I'm going to have to ask you to leave and rejoin the others."

My geriatric football fantasy, interrupted by a security guard, had come to an end. I didn't take offense. He was courteous and was just doing his job. He had no idea who I was or, more accurately, what I once was and seemed almost embarrassed at having to roust my ass out of there.

My time as a football player was past. I would never suit up for the Honolulu blue and silver again, and this crowd would never cheer for me. Ever. I didn't bother looking away, making no attempt at hiding my watery eyes and tear-streaked cheeks.

Epilogue

The moon, four days beyond full but still looming large on the horizon, started its nightly trek across the ecliptic. It rose like some giant Hollywood prop, seemingly too orange, too large, too surreal to be authentic. It cleared the distant hardwood forest of Round Lake's far south-eastern shore rapidly, showing its full girth in only a few minutes. It reflected off the now-still water, sending an iridescent band of pink straight toward our fire.

The fire, burning in a sunken pit by the water's edge, roared on. It had been lit the previous Wednesday afternoon to mark our arrival. We all pitched in, keeping it burning continuously during our stay, fueling it with native logs of dried sugar maple, oak, basswood, and beech. Tonight was our last night together, and after we all went to bed, it would finally be allowed to burn itself out and mark the end of the summer of 2002 (for us anyway) as well as our time together.

The next day my wife, Katherine, our two kids, and I would begin the long trek, via our old Ford pickup, back to our Northern California home. Rich Strenger, his wife, Karen, and their newborn baby girl would return to their suburban Detroit home in the morning as well. Rob and Debbie Rubick, our hosts for the last five days, would remain at their retreat in the Upper Peninsula of Michigan with their three kids for a few more days before returning to their home, also in the suburban Detroit area.

The days were spent carefree, with the kids dictating most of the action. We tubed behind Rob's boat, fished, shot guns from Duke's

(Rob's dad) extensive arsenal, swam, and hiked. The summer nights, which came late and were short-lived in this higher-latitude location, were reserved for adult fun. The six of us drank, ate, and talked well into the night, our stamina buoyed by our outrageous stories and recollections.

Although we brought each other up-to-date on our current activities, most of the talk centered around the time when we guys played for the National Football League's Detroit Lions. The six of us were good friends back then, and it had been too long since we had all gotten together.

The stories came fast and furious, and our laughter echoed around the lake, off the trees, and across the water. Rob and Debbie's neighbors must have thought us supermen and -women, partying and carrying on for four straight nights now without a break. To their credit, no ill words were ever spoken by them.

I for one was sad that it was coming to an end. Living where I do, far away from most of my old teammates, I rarely get a chance these days to see them or talk about my past life as a football player.

It felt good. *Real* good. Therapeutic even. And it gave me the spark to write this book. I will always be grateful for those nights. And grateful for all those incredible memories—in high school, college, and the pros—that the game of football allowed me to experience.

That's what inspired me to write this book. The memories. It certainly wasn't because I was the best football player, or even the best offensive lineman, ever to play the game. I wasn't. I never won a Super Bowl, but then, a very small percentage of NFL players ever do. And I'm never going to get elected into the pro football Hall of Fame.

I did, however, play the game full-tilt boogie—all out *all* the time— with every shred of my body and soul. I summoned emotions from deep within, striving to play the best game possible with the same fierce intensity each and every week. I was devastated when we lost and overjoyed when we won. Some games were among the best experiences of my life. At other times they had me testing the deep, dark, murky waters of despair, wondering not only if I could measure up but whether I would survive.

I believe this is the way the game was meant to be played—what the game of football is all about. It was my hope to capture that essence with my words.

I tried to portray as honestly and forthrightly as possible what it's like to play the game of football, at *any* level. I hope that those of you who played the game could relate and those of you that didn't now have a better understanding of what it's like.

Mainly, though, this book is a celebration of the people with whom I played the game, the colorful personalities I've crossed paths with over the years. What a truly incredible cast of characters! I'm blessed to have known each and every one of them. If this book had been just about me, it would have probably bored you to tears.

If you are a football fan, many of the names mentioned in this book you instantly recognized. But most, like mine, aren't household names but nonetheless are the people who helped make football the great game it is today.

Ultimately, that's what I miss most about football—the guys. It's not the spotlight, the glory, the screaming fans, or even the money. And it certainly isn't training camp. It's the guys. I hope I was able to portray to you how special all the individuals with whom I played and trained, at every level, are to me.

I currently coach football, and I try and pound home the same message week after week. It's a message that was told to me by older, wiser men when I was playing, and I'm glad I listened to them, even though it wasn't crystal clear at the time like it is now, years later.

Every football game you play—whether you realize it at the time or not—is a very precious commodity. Embrace it, let your emotions run free, but most importantly, give it your best effort. Because you *will* remember them—all of them. Above all, relish the bonds you make with your teammates, through off-season training, summer camp, seemingly endless practices and repetition, and, finally, the games.

Ah, the games. Those emotionally charged, adrenaline-pumping, insane games, where an entire gamut of emotions can be run in just a few hours. And it doesn't matter whether you play in front of a handful of people on Friday night, thousands on a Saturday afternoon, or seventy-five thousand fans and millions more on television on a Sunday.

They're all the same game.

Keep the fire burning.

Index

Index

Mornhinweg, Marty, 183
Morrison, Jim, 128, 131
Motrin, 46
Mott, Steve, 162–63
MRI, precursor to, 53
Muir, Bill, 48, 159
Murray, Eddie, 164–69
myelography, 53–54

Namath, Joe, 103–8
New Orleans Saints, 20–23
New York Jets, 84, 94, 97
NFL (National Football League),
   94–101
Nittany Lion Inn, 81
Novocaine, 163, 165

Oakland University, 2
Oceania, 9
offensive linemen, "meetings"
   of, 108–12
Ohio, 148–50
Ohio State University, 150–52
Old Carwood Grove, 117
Oleksa, Mark "Whitey," 49

Pankey, Irv, 193
Parcells, Bill, 170
Paterno, Joe
   ability to remember, 76–77
   disappointment of, 84–87
   on East-West Shrine Game,
      95

initial contact with, 75–76
and plane assignments, 169
playing for, 82–88
recruiting by, 77–78, 81
on uniforms, 172
vs. University of Michigan,
   171–72
Pendell, Tim, 174–76, 179–81
Penn State University
   vs. Alabama in Sugar Bowl,
      89–91, 184
   freshman year at, 148
   initial contact with, 75–76
   vs. Ohio State, 150–52
   plane assignments, 169
   reasons for choosing, 81–82
   recruiting by, 80–82
   vs. University of Michigan,
      171–72
Perry, William "the Refrigerator,"
   157–60
Pittsburgh Steelers, 44
Pontiac Silverdome, 23, 45–46,
   61–69, 124–31
Pro Bowl, 101
Pureifory, Dave
   at camp, 1, 10, 12–14
   friendship with, 16
   as part of "Silver Rush," 112
   on smoke in Silverdome, 23
   toughness of, 6–7

quarterbacks, 111, 158–59

Index

University of Alabama, 83, 86, 89–91, 184

University of Michigan, 79–80, 171–72

USFL (United States Football League), 16

Valium, 55

Vernaglia, Kip, 24–26, 34–37, 49–50, 184

Villipiano, Phil, 103, 105

Walsh, Bill, 15

weight room, 179–80

Wenner, Jerry, 142–43, 185

West Virginia University, 85–86

Whelan, Mike, 134, 170–71

Whitehall High School, 182

Whiteknight, Billy, 121

White, Randy, 130–31

White, Reggie, 113

Wilson Borough High School, 141–48

Winslow, Kellen, 93

Woodcock, John "Woody," 112, 193

World Series, 1988, 96

Xylocaine, 163, 165

YMCA, 120–24

Youngblood, Jack, 113

ZZ Top, 75